1200 WORDS

for the

SSAT & ISEE

For Private and Independent School Admissions

Gaëlle Pierre-Louis

ISBN: 0-692-60549-5
ISBN 13: 978-0-692-60549-3

Library of Congress Control Number: 2016930078

Publisher: The Pierre Review, Delaware, New Jersey

Dedication

I dedicate this book to my parents and siblings, my mentors and teachers at the Lawrenceville School who pushed me to reach high in my academic goals, and, last but not least, to the students in the Areté Prep Program who have inspired me during the summer of 2013.

Preface:

1200 Words for the SSAT & ISEE aims to prepare students in the 4th-11th grade for the verbal section of the Secondary School Admission Test (SSAT) and the Independent School Entrance Exam (ISEE). The book is organized alphabetically with words from A to Z. It includes up to 12 quizzes designed to reinforce knowledge of key words throughout the book. These two examinations are prerequisite for admission into private independent and boarding schools, and a high score shows these schools that the students are prepared to engaged in rigourous coursework.

When I started studying for the SSAT, I compiled these vocabulary words to help me with my studies. I passed these words down to my peers and my siblings, and they also found them incredibly helpful in their preparations. Also, students should study parts of words such as prefixes, suffixes, roots or stems. By expanding their learning of key vocabulary words, they will feel more confident, prepared, and ultimately score higher on the SSAT & ISEE verbal section. In addition, these words will be the foundation which they can build upon as they prepare to sit through the SAT college examination in the future.

About the Author:

Gaëlle Pierre-Louis is completing her studies at Georgetown University's School of Foreign Service in Washington, D.C.. Prior to attending Georgetown University, she attended the Lawrenceville School in Lawrenceville, New Jersey.

Abate (verb) To become weaker; to decrease in strength.
▪ The pilot waited for the wind to abate before flying the plane.
To reduce in degree, in force, or in intensity; to put an end to; nullify.
(Synonym) Fall, Let up, Lessen.

Abdicate (verb) To renounce a throne, high office, dignity; to give up the position of being king or queen.
▪ King Edward VIII chose to abdicate his throne in December 1936.
To fail to do what is required by a duty or responsibility; to relinquish.
(Synonym) Step down, Quit, Resign. (Antonym) Accept.

Abduct (verb) To take someone away from a place by force.
▪ The militants plan to abduct a group of girls from their school in Nigeria.
(Synonym) Kidnap, Seize, Capture.

Abet (verb) To help, encourage, or support someone in a criminal act; to actively second and assist.
▪ He was arrested for abetting his girlfriend's unlawful actions.
(Synonym) Urge, Instigate, Prompt. (Antonym) Deter.

Abhor (verb) To detest; to regard with extreme disgust and hatred.
▪ The human rights movement abhors slavery.
(Synonym) Dislike, Loathe, Despise.

Abjure (verb) To renounce under oath; to reject solemnly.
▪ Michael abjured his former religious beliefs.
(Synonym) Repudiate, Abnegate, Deny.

Abode (noun) The place where someone lives; a temporary stay, sojourn.
▪ My parents bought a house in the Poconos for a summer vacation abode.
(Synonym) Dwelling, One's home, Domicile.

Abolish (verb) To end the observance or effect of; to put an end to.
▪ In 1865, the Thirteenth Amendment to the US Constitution abolished slavery.
(Synonym) Stop, Eradicate, Eliminate.

Abominable (adjective) Very bad or unpleasant.
▪ He was arrested for committing an abominable crime.
(Synonym) Horrendous, Terrible, Dreadful.

Abrasive (adjective) Causing damage or wear by rubbing, grinding, or scraping; of or relating to abrasion.
▪ The whitening soap had an abrasive effect on skin.
Having a rough quality; very unpleasant or irritating.
(Synonym) Rough, Coarse, Harsh.

Abridge (verb) To shorten by omission of words without sacrifice of sense.
- His professor asked him to abridge the length of his essay from 750 to 500 words.
(Synonym) Reduce, Condense, Abbreviate. (Antonym) Expand.

Abrupt (adjective) Very sudden and not expected.
- The abrupt stop of the car shocked everyone.
(Synonym) Brusque, Hasty, Rushed. (Antonym) Gradual.

Abscond (verb) To go away or escape.
- The banker absconded with the money he stole from the bank.
(Synonym) Leave, Run away, Depart.

Absolute (adjective) Not limited in any way; free from doubt; complete and total.
- Nobody can predict the future with absolute certainty.
(Synonym) Definite, Certain, Entire.

Absolve (verb) To make someone free from guilt, blame or responsibility; to clear.
- The government has a program that absolves students of repaying their loans.
(Synonym) Pardon, Forgive, Excuse. (Antonym) Punish.

Absorb (verb) To suck up or drink in a liquid; soak up.
- I placed a sponge mat in front of the kitchen sink to absorb water.
To take up the whole interest or attention of someone.
- I was so absorbed by the lecture that I didn't hear the bell ring.
(Synonym) Captivate, Fascinate, Grasp.

Abstain (verb) To refrain from; to choose not to vote.
- Children should abstain from drinking alcohol.
(Synonym) Desist, Withdraw, Withhold.

Abstemious (adjective) Marked by restraint, especially in the consumption of food or alcohol.
- My father is an abstemious drinker.
(Synonym) Moderate, Self-disciplined, Temperate.

Absurd (adjective) Extremely silly, foolish, or unreasonable; completely ridiculous.
- It is absurd to think that you can wear flip-flops during the winter.
(Synonym) Futile, Bizarre, Strange. (Antonym) Reasonable.

Abyss (noun) A hole so deep or a space so great that it cannot be measured.
- The abyss of the ocean.
(Synonym) Hole, Depth, Void.

Accede (verb) To agree to a request or a demand; to enter a high office or position.
- Upon the king's death, Princess Elizabeth acceded to the throne in 1952.
(Synonym) Attain, Assent, Consent. (Antonym) Reject.

Access (noun) The means to reach or enter; freedom or ability to use something.
- The local public library provides free internet access.
(Synonym) Admission, Admittance, Entrance.

Acclaim (noun) Strong approval or praise.
- The memoir *I Know Why the Caged Bird Sings* by Maya Angelou drew wide acclaim.
(Synonym) Compliment, Applause, Commendation.

Accord (noun) A formal or official agreement; a situation in which people agree.
- The two warring countries reached an accord for peace.
(Synonym) Settlement, Agreement, Pact.

Accrue (verb) To increase; to accumulate.
- I place my retirement money in stocks so that it can accrue dividends.
(Synonym) Grow, Amass, Add.

Accurate (adjective) Free from mistakes or errors; able to produce results that are correct.
- I want you to give me an accurate answer.
(Synonym) Precise, Exact, True.

Acquaintance (noun) A person whom one knows but who is not a particularly close friend.
- My mother ran into an acquaintance at the mall.
(Synonym) Associate, Colleague, Social contact. (Antonym) Stranger.

Acquiesce (verb) To accept, agree, comply, or give consent by staying silent or by not arguing.
- She acquiesced to her mom's request to take out the trash.
(Synonym) Concede, Go along with, Concede. (Antonym) Resist.

Acquire (verb) To come to own something, especially through your own effort; gain a new skill, ability.
- While interning in Paris, she quickly acquired fluency in French.
(Synonym) Obtain, Attain, Procure.

Acrid (adjective) Bitter, strong, and harsh or unpleasantly pungent in taste or smell; irritating.
- The acrid smell in the basement made me feel sick.
(Synonym) Acerbic, Sour, Sharp. (Antonym) Pleasant, Savory.

Acumen (noun) The ability to think clearly and make good decisions. Keen insight or discernment.
- Ronnie's business acumen gained her respect in the company.
(Synonym) Intelligence, Judgment, Expertise.

Ad-lib (verb) To deliver spontaneously; to improvise; to make up words or music in a performance instead of saying or playing something that has been planned.
- Some of the best parts of his speech were ad-libbed.
(Synonym) To utter while unprepared, Impromptu, Make up on the spot.

Adage (noun) An old familiar saying that expresses a general truth.
- My father like the adage "an ounce of prevention is worth a pound of cure."
(Synonym) Proverb, Maxim, Saying.

Adamant (adjective) Not willing to change an opinion or decision; very determined; not giving in.
- My cousin is an adamant defender of human rights.
(Synonym) Obstinate, Inflexible, Stubborn. (Antonym) Compliant.

Addition (noun) The act or process of adding something; the arithmetic operation of summing.
- Last month, my brother welcomed baby Xavier; he's the new addition to the family.
(Synonym) Inclusion, Accumulation, Supplement.

Adequate (adjective) Enough for some need or requirement; good enough.
- I need an adequate amount of flour to finish the cupcakes.
Of a quality that is acceptable but not better than acceptable.
- Your grades are adequate, but they need improvement.
(Synonym) Passable, Satisfactory, Tolerable. (Antonym) Inadequate.

Adhere (verb) To stick to something; to attach firmly to something.
- Students need to adhere to the school's rules and regulations.
(Synonym) Observe, Follow, Obey.

Admonish (verb) To speak to someone in a way that expresses disapproval or criticism.
- We were admonished by our parents for having failing grades on our report cards.
(Synonym) Reprove, Reprimand, Reproach. (Antonym) Praise.

Adorn (verb) to make something more attractive by adding something beautiful.
- My parents adorned the kitchen's countertop with new tiles.
(Synonym) Garnish, Decorate, Enhance. (Antonym) Strip.

Adulterate (verb) To make food or drink impure or weaker by adding another substance of poor quality to it.
- John's milk is said to be adulterated with a toxic substance called melamine.
(Synonym) Dilute, Contaminate, Pollute. (Antonym) Purify.

Adversary (noun) One that contends with, opposes, or resists; an enemy or opponent.
- My friend consistently beats her adversary in their annual tennis match.
(Synonym) Challenger, Antagonist, Rival. (Antonym) Supporter.

Adversity (noun) A difficult situation or condition; hard times; misfortune or tragedy.
- It is through adversity that you will discover your true friends.
(Synonym) Hardship, Danger, Harsh conditions. (Antonym) Privilege.

Affable (adjective) Being pleasant and at ease in talking to others; friendly.

▪ My mother is a lively and affable woman.
(Synonym) Cordial, Gregarious, Sociable.

Affinity (noun) The state of sharing similar qualities, ideas, or interests; a natural connection.
▪ My son and his friend Zack have an affinity for the sport of basketball.
(Synonym) Attraction, Resemblance, Kinship. (Antonym) Difference.

Affirm (verb) To state positively; to say that something is true in a confident way.
▪ The woman affirmed that she saw the two men jumping over her gate.
To decide that the judgment of another court is correct.
▪ People are asked to affirm that they will tell the truth in a court of law.
(Synonym) Confirm, Support, Validate.

Affluent (adjective) Having a large amount of money and owning many expensive things.
▪ She has affluent friends who share their wealth with those who are less well off.
Having a generously sufficient and typically increasing supply of material possessions.
(Synonym) Wealthy, Prosperous, Comfortable. (Antonym) Poor.

Agenda (noun) A list or outline of things to be done or talked about.
▪ You need to set your agenda before announcing the meeting.
(Synonym) Schedule, Plan, Itinerary.

Aggrandizement (noun) Increase in power rank or wealth; to appear greater than is the case.
▪ She has acquainted herself with the affluent and the famous for her personal aggrandizement.
(Synonym) Exaggeration, Glorification, Boasting. (Antonym) Understatement.

Aggregate (noun) The collection of many units into one body; to combine into one mass or whole.
▪ In the aggregate, a country's gains from trade may not be very large.
(Synonym) Combination, Collection, Total.

Aghast (adjective) Struck with terror, surprise, or horror; shocked and upset.
▪ My sister stood aghast at the sight of ghost costumes on Halloween.
(Synonym) Amazed, Horrified, Stunned.

Agile (adjective) Smart, clever; marked by ready ability to move quickly and easily.
▪ My brother is the most agile athlete on the basketball team.
(Synonym) Nimble, Dexterous, Responsive. (Antonym) Clumsy.

Agog (adjective) Full of interest or excitement.
▪ My siblings were agog with joy over their new toys on Christmas Day.
(Synonym) Surprised, Enthusiastic, Eager. (Antonym) Uninterested.

Ailment (noun) A bodily disorder or chronic disease; a sickness or illness.

▪ She was treated for a variety of ailments, including diabetes and high blood pressure.
(Synonym) Weakness, Condition, Infirmity.

Alias (noun) An assumed or a false name that a person sometimes uses.
▪ Andrew Spencer traveled to Europe under the alias Conrad.
(Synonym) Pseudonym, Other name, Otherwise known as.

Alien (adjective) not familiar or like other things you have known; from another country, foreign.
▪ The cultural etiquettes of the Caribbean islands were alien to the foreigners.
(Synonym) Strange, Extraterrestrial, Unknown.

Align (verb) To arrange things so they form a line or are in proper position; to bring into line.
▪ The painting on the wall is not properly aligned with the other paintings.

Allegation (noun) A statement not supported by proof that usually accuses someone of having done something wrong or illegal.
▪ Her allegation was that I stole the utensils from the school's cafeteria.
(Synonym) Accusation, Charge, Fabrication.

Alleviate (verb) To reduce the pain or trouble; to make something less painful, difficult, or severe.
▪ These pills will alleviate the pain.
(Synonym) Lessen, Help, Relieve. (Antonym) Aggravate.

Allot (verb) To give out as a share or portion.
▪ Each heir will be allotted a portion of the land.
(Synonym) Allocate, Assign, Distribute.

Ally (verb) To join or enter into an alliance; to form a friendship.
▪ They have allied against their opponents.
(Synonym) Affiliate, Associate, Cooperate. (Antonym) Oppose.

Aloof (adjective) Not Friendly or outgoing; at a distance.
▪ Connor held himself aloof from his classmates.
(Synonym) Reserved, Cold, Indifferent. (Antonym) Friendly.

Alter (verb) To change something partly but not completely.
▪ She made a decision that will alter her life forever.
To make a change to a piece of clothing so that it will fit better.
▪ I will buy the dress and have it altered at the dry cleaners.
(Synonym) Modify, Amend, Adjust.

Amass (verb) To collect or gather together.
▪ We amassed ample information on the subject before writing the final thesis.

(Synonym) Assemble, Accrue, Accumulate.

Amaze (verb) To fill someone with wonder; to show or cause astonishment; to surprise.
- I was always amazed at Mona Lisa's beauty.
(Synonym) Bewilder, Astound, Stun.

Ambiguous (adjective) Able to be understood in more than one way; having more than one possible meaning.
- Due to the ambiguous nature of the question, it was difficult to choose the right answer.
(Synonym) Obscure, Unclear, Confusing. (Antonym) Clear.

Ambivalent (adjective) Uncertainty as to which approach to follow; having different feelings such as love and hate at the same time; continual fluctuation between one thing and its opposite.
- After high school, my sister was ambivalent about whether to go to college or go into the workforce.
(Synonym) Undecided, Hesitant, Unsure. (Antonym) Decisive.

Ambulatory (adjective) Of or relating to walking; moving from place to place; itinerant.
- Adele works in the Ambulatory Surgery Department.

Ameliorate (verb) To make better, less painful.
- Ginger tea should help ameliorate your horrible cough.
(Synonym) Improve, Enhance, Upgrade.

Amend (verb) To change some of the words and the meaning of a law or document.
- The constitution has been amended multiple times.
(Synonym) Adjust, Modify, Improve.

Amiable (adjective) Being friendly, sociable, pleasant, and congenial; generally agreeable.
- She had an amiable conversation with her friend.
(Synonym) Genial, Good-natured, Affable.

Amicable (adjective) Showing a polite and friendly desire to avoid disagreement and argument.
- They reached an amicable agreement.
(Synonym) Harmonious, Good Humored, Cordial. (Antonym) Disagreeable.

Amoral (adjective) Showing no concern about whether behavior is morally right or wrong.
- The elected official's amoral personality is not commendable.
(Synonym) Unethical, Immoral, Dishonorable. (Antonym) Principled.

Amorphous (adjective) Having no definite form or clear shape; shapeless. Lacking organization or unity.
- Spencer needs to practice his writing to ameliorate his amorphous style of writing.
(Synonym) Formless, Nebulous, Vague. (Antonym) Defined.

Ample (adjective) Having or providing enough or more than enough of what is needed.
- You will have ample time to finish the test.
(Synonym) Abundant, Copious, Plentiful. (Antonym) Insufficient.

Amulet (noun) A charm or an ornament worn to protect the person wearing it against illness, bad luck, or witchcraft.
- Anna wore an amulet as her lucky charm every time she performed in front of an audience.
(Synonym) Talisman, Charm.

Anarchy (noun) A situation of confusion and wild behavior in which the people in a country, group, or organization are not controlled by rules or laws.
- When authority is not enforced, it leads to anarchy.
(Synonym) Disorder, Chaos, Mayhem. (Antonym) Order.

Anchor (noun) A heavy device that is attached to a boat or ship to hold it in place; someone who reads the news on a television broadcast, as in anchorman or anchorwoman.
- His uncle works as a television news anchor.
(Synonym) Journalist, Broadcaster, Commentator.

Animosity (noun) A strong feeling of dislike or hatred.
- We put aside our personal animosities so that we could work together.
(Synonym) Hostility, Loathing, Antagonism.

Antagonize (verb) A person who is against; to act in opposition to; counteract.
- Her arrogant comments antagonized the students.
(Synonym) Provoke, Annoy, Upset.

Antediluvian (adjective) Something that is very old and out of date.
- My grandparents lived in an antediluvian mansion in Spain.
(Synonym) Prehistoric, Ancient, Primitive. (Antonym) Modern.

Anticipate (verb) To think of something that will or might happen in the future.
- They do not anticipate any security hazards.
To expect or look ahead to something with pleasure; to look forward to something.
- I eagerly anticipated my daughter's arrival from college for Thanksgiving.
(Synonym) Predict, Antedate, Foresee.

Antidote (noun) A substance that stops the harmful effects of a poison.
- Exercise is a good antidote for anxiety.
(Synonym) Remedy, Antitoxin, Medicine.

Antithesis (noun) The state of two things that are directly opposite to each other.
- Poverty's antithesis is wealth.
(Synonym) Converse, Contrast, Reverse.

Anxiety (noun) Fear or nervousness about what might happen.

- On the day of the exam, Felix went to the hospital suffering from test anxiety.
(Synonym) Worry, Concern, Apprehension. (Antonym) Calm.

Apathetic (adjective) Not showing much emotion or interest; no feeling; indifferent.
- Young students today are becoming increasingly apathetic toward social issues.
(Synonym) Unconcerned, Lethargic, Lazy. (Antonym) Energetic.

Apathy (noun) Lack of feeling or emotion; impassiveness; lack of interest or concern; indifference.
- They had to recall the product because of consumers' apathy toward the new design.
(Synonym) Lethargy, Boredom, Laziness.

Aplomb (noun) Complete and confident composure, skill, or self-assurance; poise shown especially in a difficult situation.
- She speaks French and German with equal aplomb.
(Synonym) Ease, Style, Assurance. (Antonym) Awkwardness.

Apologist (noun) A person who defends or supports something such as a religion, cause, or organization that is being criticized or attacked by other people.
- The speaker was viewed as an apologist for the Islamic religion.
(Synonym) Protector, Advocator, Ally.

Apparatus (noun) A tool, material, or piece of equipment used for specific job or activities.
- My son plays golf. Thus, I will buy him the apparatus for golf.
The organization or system used for doing or operating something singular.
- The voters demanded the downsizing of the government apparatus.
(Synonym) Device, Mechanism, Gear.

Apparition (noun) A ghost or spirit of a dead person.
- While Emily was working late in her office, she witnessed an apparition.
(Synonym) Vision, Specter, Phantom.

Apprehension (noun) Fear that something bad is going to happen; a feeling of being worried about the future.
- The thought of moving to Ohio fills me with apprehension.
(Synonym) Anxiety, Dread, Concern.

Approve (verb) The belief that something is good or acceptable; to express a favorable opinion of; to judge favorably.
- I am happy that my application for the loan has been approved.
(Synonym) Favor, Support, Endorse.

Aptitude (noun) A natural ability; talent; capacity for learning.
- Michelle has a great aptitude for learning languages; she speaks English, French, Spanish, and German.
(Synonym) Skill, Gift, Propensity.

Aquatic (adjective) Play in or on water; growing, living, or done in water.
- I practice aquatic sports such as swimming and diving.
(Synonym) Sea, River, Marine.

Ardor (noun) A strong feeling of energy or eagerness; warmth of feeling; a strong feeling of love.
- He is campaigning for the governor with zeal and ardor.
(Synonym) Zeal, Fervor, Passion. (Antonym) Indifference.

Arduous (adjective) Very difficult; marked by great labor or effort; hard to accomplish or achieve.
- It was an arduous expedition to climb up Mount Everest last summer.
(Synonym) Demanding, Strenuous, Exhausting.

Arid (adjective) Very dry; having very little rain or water; lacking feeling or interest.
- Once the irrigation system ceased operating, the land became arid desert once again.
(Synonym) Parched, Scorched, Waterless.

Aristocracy (noun) An upper class that is usually based on birth and is richer and more powerful than the rest of a society.
The highest social class in some countries; people thought of as being better than the rest of the community.
- Members of the French aristocracy enjoyed privileged lives.
(Synonym) Nobility, Gentry, Elite.

Armada (noun) A large fleet of warships.
- The Spanish Armada was defeated by an English fleet that by some measures was inferior.
(Synonym) Squadron, Flotilla, Navy.

Articulate (adjective) Able to express clearly and effectively in speech or writing.
- She is very intelligent and articulate.
(Synonym) Eloquent, Fluent, Expressive.

Aspiration (noun) Something that a person wants very much to achieve.
- What are your aspirations for the future?
The act of pronouncing the sound of a breath or the letter *h*.
- In US English, the letter *h* in the word *herb* is not aspirated unless *Herb* is used as a person's name.
(Synonym) Goal, Hope, Objective.

Assess (verb) To make a judgment about something.
- After Sandy hit the coast, the officials assessed the town's need for aid.
To officially say what the amount, value, or rate of something is.
- The car dealership assessed the value of my old car at $1,500.
To tax or charge; to require a person or business to pay a particular amount of money.
- The company was assessed $12 million in fines for polluting the river.

(Synonym) Measure, Evaluate, Size up.

Assist (verb) To give support or help.
- The trained dog assists the blind man in crossing the street every day.
(Synonym) Aid, Lend a hand, Give succor to. (Antonym) Hinder.

Assistance (noun) The act of helping or assisting someone; help or support.
- The United States provided financial assistance to Haiti after the earthquake.
(Synonym) Service, Backing, Aid.

Astound (verb) To cause a feeling of great surprise or wonder in someone; to fill with bewilderment.
- I was astounded by her ability to play Mozart so well.
(Synonym) Amaze, Astonish, Stun.

Asylum (noun) Protection given by a government to someone who has left another country in order to escape harm.
- The president was granted asylum in Europe after he was overthrown.
A hospital where people who are mentally ill are cared for, especially for long periods of time; a mental hospital.
(Synonym) Refuge, Sanctuary, Retreat.

Atone (verb) To do something good as a way to show sorrow about doing something bad.
- My mother prays often to atone for the sins of the whole family.
To supply satisfaction for; expiate; to make amends.
(Synonym) Compensate, Apologize, Repent.

Attitude (noun) The way one thinks and feels about someone or something.
- Attitudes toward birth and death vary from culture to culture.
A feeling or way of thinking that affects a person's behavior.
- She has a positive attitude toward her work.
A particular way of positioning your body or figure; posture.
- At church, the priest places his palms together in an attitude of prayer.
(Synonym) Manner, Viewpoint, Disposition.

Attribute (noun) A usually good quality or feature that someone or something has.
- Both candidates possess the attributes that we look for in a leader.
(Synonym) Aspect, Characteristic, Trait.

Audacity (noun) A confident and daring quality that is often seen as shocking or rude; intrepid boldness or arrogant disregard of normal restraints.
- Disraeli once said, "Success is the child of audacity."
(Synonym) Courage, Bravery, Boldness. (Antonym) Cowardice.

Audible (adjective) Heard or able to be heard.
- I was hoping that her unpleasant comment was not audible.

(Synonym) Perceptible, Distinct, Noticeable.

Auspicious (adjective) Showing or suggesting that future success is likely; promising success.
- It is an auspicious time to start business.
(Synonym) Favorable, Promising.

Austere (adjective) Having a serious, stern, unapproachable, and unfriendly quality; cold in appearance or manner.
- My fifth-grade teacher has an austere demeanor.
Giving little or no scope for pleasure; simple and harsh.
- They lived an austere life in the country.
(Synonym) Somber, Rigid, Strict. (Antonym) Easygoing, Comfortable.

Austerity (noun) A simple and plain quality.
- In my brother's house, the austerity of the furniture is not inviting.
A situation in which there is not much money, and it is spent only on things that are necessary; enforced or extreme economy.
- After the depression, this family lived through years of austerity.
(Synonym) Severity, Strictness, Self-discipline.

Authentic (adjective) Real, not copied; true and accurate.
- I bought an authentic bag in Paris, and as proof the store gave me a signature from the designer.
Made to be or look just like an original so as to reproduce essential features.
- She bought an authentic painting of Queen Isabelle's castle.
(Synonym) True, Accurate, Genuine. (Antonym) Fake.

Authority (noun) The power or right to direct or control; power to influence or command thought, opinion, or behavior.
- The department managers are the only people who have the authority to sign vacation checks.
Government or persons in command who have power to make decisions and enforce rules and laws.
- Local authorities are investigating the crime.
(Synonym) Expert, Ability, Influence.

Automatic (adjective) Having controls that allow something to work or happen without being directly controlled by a person.
- The supermarket's entrance doors run automatically.
Happening or done without deliberate thought or effort.
- She always has an automatic reply.
(Synonym) Spontaneous, Involuntary, Impulsive.

Avarice (noun) Excessive or insatiable desire for wealth or gain; a strong desire to have money; greed.
- The corporate world is plagued by avarice and a thirst for power.

(Synonym) Avidity, Materialism, Acquisitiveness.

Aversion (noun) A strong feeling of not liking something, with a desire to avoid or turn from it.
▪ My classmate Evelyn has an aversion to vegetables.
(Synonym) Repugnance, Distaste, Dislike.

Avert (verb) To turn one's eyes or gaze away or aside in avoidance; to look away.
▪ She had to avert her eyes at the sight of the accident.
To prevent something bad from happening.
▪ My dad did construction work on his backyard to avert the flood from coming into the basement.
(Synonym) Deter, Prevent, Turn away.

QUIZ# 1.- MATCH EACH WORD IN THE FIRST COLUMN WITH ITS SYNONYM IN THE SECOND COLUMN. CHECK YOUR ANSWERS IN THE BACK OF THE BOOK.

1. abate	a. reserved
2. abdicate	b. favorable
3. abjure	c. shapeless
4. abridge	d. greed
5. abyss	e. decrease
6. acquiesce	f. shorten
7. adage	g. plentiful
8. aloof	h. renounce
9. amiable	i. hole
10. ample	j. help
11. apathy	k. resign
12. amorphous	l. indifference
13. assist	m. friendly
14. auspicious	n. agree
15. avarice	o. proverb

Bailiff (noun) An officer in a court of law who helps the judge control the people in the courtroom; someone hired by a sheriff to take legal documents to people and to take away possessions when people cannot pay for them; one who manages the land or farm and property of another person.
▪ Arnold prevented the bailiff from taking away his land.
(Synonym) Court officer, Evictor, Law officer.

Ban (verb) To forbid; to prohibit the use, performance, or distribution of something, especially by legal means.
▪ The mayor banned smoking in all public restaurants.
(Synonym) Interdict, Bar, Veto.

Barter (verb) To exchange products or services for other things instead of money; to trade by exchanging one commodity for another.
▪ The farmer bartered a dozen eggs for a pair of shoes.
(Synonym) Negotiate, Trade, Bargain.

Bashful (adjective) Uneasy in the presence of others; afraid to talk to people because of a lack of confidence; socially shy or timid.
▪ Kathy was very bashful when meeting First Lady Obama last summer.
(Synonym) Self-conscious, Reticent, Reserved. (Antonym) Bold.

Basin (noun) A kitchen sink; a large bowl that is used for mixing, cooking, or serving food.
▪ The chef broke two eggs into a basin.
(Synonym) Bowl, Sink.

Befriend (verb) To become or act as a friend to someone.
▪ I befriended the new student to make her at ease.
(Synonym) Approach, Help, Support.

Beget (verb) To cause something to happen or exist; to produce, especially as an effect or outgrowth.
▪ Wealth begets wealth.
To become the mother or father of someone; to procreate as the mother or the father.
▪ My aunt died without begetting an heir.
(Synonym) Create, Bring, Lead to.

Behave (verb) To act in a particular manner; to act in an acceptable way; to conduct oneself properly.
▪ These children are rude, and they behave badly.
To function, react, or move in a particular way.
▪ The economist is studying how the market behaves when supply and demand change.
(Synonym) Be good, Perform, Do the right thing.

Belittle (verb) To describe a person or thing as little or unimportant; disparage.
▪ She complained that her manager belittled her work performance.
(Synonym) Depreciate, Put down. (Antonym) Praise.

Bellicose (adjective) Having or showing a tendency to argue or fight; favoring or inclined to start quarrels or wars.
▪ He has a bellicose behavior.
(Synonym) Belligerent, Aggressive, Warlike. (Antonym) Compliant.

Belligerent (noun) A group or country that is fighting a war; feeling or showing readiness to fight.
▪ The hockey fans became belligerent after their team lost.
(Synonym) Quarrelsome, Argumentative, Combative. (Antonym) Easygoing.

Benefactor (noun) Someone who helps another person or group by giving money.
▪ A wealthy benefactor helped Victoria pay for her graduate studies.
(Synonym) Sponsor, Contributor, Patron.

Beneficial (adjective) Producing good or helpful results or effects; producing benefits.
▪ Good eating habits and regular exercise have many beneficial health effects.
(Synonym) Advantageous, Useful, Helpful.

Benefit (noun) A good or helpful result or effect.
▪ The concert proceeds will go to the fund that benefits the children of low-income families.
(Synonym) Profit, Assistance, Advantage.

Benevolent (adjective) Kind and generous; having a desire to do good.
▪ He volunteers in several benevolent societies and charitable organizations.
(Synonym) Compassionate, Charitable, Giving. (Antonym) Malevolent.

Benign (adjective) Not causing death or serious injury; not becoming cancerous; harmless.
▪ We were happy to hear that the tumor was benign.
(Synonym) Nonthreatening, Gentle. (Antonym) Malignant.

Berate (verb) To yell at someone; to scold in a loud and angry way.
▪ My mother berated me for staying out too late.
(Synonym) Rebuke, Criticize, Reprimand.

Bias (noun) A tendency to believe that some people or ideas are better than others that usually results in treating some people unfairly.
▪ The law prohibits bias in the workplace on the basis of race, color, national origin, sex, age, or disability.
(Synonym) Prejudice, Preference, Favoritism.

Bibliography (noun) A list of materials such as books, magazines, and articles that were used in the preparation of a written work or mentioned in a text.
▪ You should include a bibliography in your written project.
(Synonym) List of books, Catalog, List of references.

Biceps (noun) A large muscle of the front of the upper arm.
▪ Philip came home with a deep bruise on his biceps.

Biodegrade (verb) To decay; capable of being slowly destroyed and broken down into very small parts by natural processes (as in bacteria etc.).
▪ Plastic bottles do not biodegrade.

Bizarre (adjective) Very unusual or strange; out of the ordinary, odd, extravagant, or eccentric in style or mode.
▪ The bearded lady wore a bizarre outfit and scared the children.
(Synonym) Inexplicable, Weird, Curious. (Antonym) Ordinary.

Blatant (adjective) Very obvious and offensive.
▪ He gave a blatant lie to the teacher for missing his homework.
(Synonym) Flagrant, Noisy, Unashamed.

Bleak (adjective) Lacking in warmth, life, or kindliness; grim; not hopeful or encouraging, depressing; not friendly.
▪ The cold rainy weather is bleak.
(Synonym) Cheerless, Dreary, Unwelcoming. (Antonym) Cheerful.

Bliss (noun) Complete happiness.
▪ People of the Christian faith pray to God for eternal bliss.
(Synonym) Joy, Ecstasy, Delight. (Antonym) Misery.

Blithe (adjective) Showing a lack of proper thought or consideration; not caring or worrying; carefree.
▪ While driving, Julia was talking on her cell phone and passed with blithe through a red light.
(Synonym) Lighthearted, Unconcerned, Happy.

Boarder (noun) A person who pays to live and have daily meals at another person's house or at a school.
▪ Gaëlle was a boarder at the Lawrenceville School.
(Synonym) Occupant, Roomer, Lodger.

Boast (verb) To express too much pride in oneself or in something one has done or achieved.
▪ The cousins boast about their new yacht.
To have something that is impressive; a cause for pride.
▪ The public high school boasts about its outstanding college matriculation lists.
(Synonym) Brag, Show off, Enjoy.

Boon (noun) Something pleasant or helpful that comes at just the right time; a benefit or advantage.
▪ I did not have any money, so it was a boon when I sold my gold chain.
(Synonym) Benefit, Gift, Blessing.

Boorish (adjective) Rude unmannerly person; resembling or befitting a boor as in crude insensitivity.
▪ His friend is boorish; he displayed bad manners.
(Synonym) Rough, Ill-mannered, Impolite. (Antonym) Well-mannered.

Booty (noun) Money or goods stolen or taken in war; a valuable gain or prize.
▪ I spend money buying booty from antiques stores.
(Synonym) Plunder, Treasure, Loot.

Botanist (noun) A scientist who studies plant life.
▪ Modern botanists study the DNA of plants.

Bound (adjective) Very likely or certain to do or to be something.
▪ Anna is bound to achieve success in her life.
▪ It is bound to be a great party.
(Synonym) Guaranteed, Compelled, Obliged.

Boundary (noun) Something such as a river, a fence, that shows where an area begins and ends.
▪ Those two trees mark the boundary of our property.
(Synonym) Border, Limit, Frontier.

Bounteous (adjective) Giving in plenty; abundant.
▪ Together we give thanks for this bounteous harvest.
(Synonym) Generous, Profuse, Ample. (Antonym) Scarce.

Bounty (noun) Good things that are given or provided freely and in large amounts.
▪ The store is filled with a bounty of fresh flowers.
A payment in the capture of an outlaw; money given as a reward for catching a criminal.
▪ They were awarded a bounty of $700 for catching the criminal.
(Synonym) Reward, Generous Gift, Prize.

Brag (verb) To talk about one's self, achievements, or family in a way that shows too much pride.
▪ Laura brags that her son goes to the most prestigious public school in the state.
A pompous or boastful statement; arrogant talk or manner; cockiness.
(Synonym) Swank, Boast, Show off.

Breach (noun) A failure to do what is required by law; failure to act in a required or promised way.
▪ If you do not do what the contract requires, you will be sued for breach of contract.
(Synonym)Violation, Infringement, Breaking. (Antonym) Compliance.

Brevity (noun) The quality of being brief such as shortness of duration or the use of few words to say something.
▪ In *Hamlet*, Polonius suggests that "brevity is the soul of wit."
The quality or fact of lasting only for a short period of time.
▪ The brevity of youth is recognized only by those older.
(Synonym) Briefness, Shortness, Succinctness.

Brittle (adjective) Easily broken or cracked, not strong; easily damaged.
- The pages of my professor textbook were very brittle.
(Synonym) Fragile, Delicate, Breakable.

Broach (verb) To introduce a subject or issue for discussion; to make known for the first time.
- He broached the idea of traveling to Thailand this spring.
(Synonym) Present, Proposed, Mentioned.

Brunt (noun) The main force; the greater part.
- The activist took the brunt of the protest.
(Synonym) Heavy part, Burden, Force.

Buffet (verb) To strike repeatedly, to blow, especially of the hand or fist; to toss about.

Buffet (noun) A meal for which different foods are placed on a table so that people can serve themselves.
- The wedding reception dinner was served buffet style.

Buffoon (noun) A stupid or foolish person who tries to be funny.
- They hired a buffoon to make a funny joke at the ceremony.
(Synonym) Comedian, Wag, Joker.

Burden (noun) To have a heavy load; something that is very difficult to accept or deal with.
- After the death of her parents, Malia had the burden of caring for her younger siblings.
(Synonym) Affliction, Duty, Responsibility.

Cacophony (noun) Unpleasant loud sounds; harsh-sounding noises.
- The orchestra's use of dissonant chords sounds like a cacophony.
(Synonym) Discord, Dissonance, Unmusicality. (Antonym) Harmony.

Cagey (adjective) Not willing to say everything that you know about something; careful to avoid being trapped; very clever.
- Officials are being cagey about saying if the president will be in town.
(Synonym) Cautious, Shrewd, Uncommunicative, Wary.

Cahier (noun) A report or memorial concerning policy, especially of a parliamentary body.
- The second article of the cahier included the abolition of slavery.

Cajole (verb) To coax or persuade, especially by flattery or false promises; to deceive with soothing words.
- My roommate cajoled me into helping him with his math homework.
(Synonym) Convince, Entice, Influence. (Antonym) Compel.

Calamity (noun) A disastrous event marked by great loss and lasting distress and suffering.
- Floods, earthquakes, volcanoes, and cyclones are calamities of nature.
(Synonym) Misfortune, Catastrophe, Tragedy.

QUIZ# 2.- MATCH EACH WORD IN THE FIRST COLUMN WITH ITS SYNONYM IN THE SECOND COLUMN. CHECK YOUR ANSWERS IN THE BACK OF THE BOOK.

1. ban	a. shortness
2. barter	b. happy
3. bashful	c. forbid
4. belligerent	d. obvious
5. bias	e. fool
6. bizarre	f. violation
7. blatant	g. abundant
8. bleak	h. shy
9. blithe	i. breakable
10. boundary	j. dreary
11. bounteous	k. trade
12. breach	l. limit
13. brevity	m. warlike
14. brittle	n. preference
15. buffoon	o. odd

Caliber (noun) Degree of excellence or importance; level of mental capacity or moral quality.
- The university will hire only professors of the highest caliber.
(Synonym) Ability, Capacity, Standard.

Calligraphy (noun) The art of making beautiful handwriting; artistic, stylized penmanship.
- Calligraphy is beautiful writing.
(Synonym) Scribble, Script, Lettering.

Calm (adjective) Not angry, upset, or excited.
- She appeared calm at the trial.
(Synonym) Peaceful, Soothing, Tranquil.

Camaraderie (noun) A feeling of good friendship among the people in a group.
- Our team has developed a real camaraderie after playing soccer for so long.
(Synonym) Fellowship, Solidarity, Comradeship. (Antonym) Enmity.

Camouflage (noun) A way of hiding something; concealment by means of disguise, especially of military equipment, by painting it or covering it with leaves or branches to make it harder to see.
▪ Soldiers use leaf-colored materials for camouflage.
Something such as color or shape that protects an animal from attack by making the animal difficult to see in the area around it.
▪ Most animals have camouflage to protect themselves from predators.
(Synonym) Cover-up, Façade, Mask.

Candid (adjective) Marked by honest sincere expression; relating to photography, showing people acting in a natural way without being posed.
▪ She received a candid snapshot from her last meeting.
Expressing opinions and feelings in an honest and sincere way; free from bias, prejudice, or malice.
▪ He gave a candid lecture about his past addiction.
(Synonym) Truthful, Frank, Straightforward.

Canine (adjective) Of or relating to dogs.
▪ German shepherds are used by the police department's canine unit.

Canopy (noun) Piece of cloth that hangs over a bed or throne as a decoration or shelter.
▪ Last summer, I bought a beautiful caravan canopy under which I will sleep outdoors.
Clear section that covers the part where the pilot sits in some airplanes.
(Synonym) Cover, Sunshade, Roof.

Cantankerous (adjective) Often angry and annoyed; difficult to deal with.
▪ My neighbor is a cantankerous old man; he is quarrelsome and disagreeable.
(Synonym) Belligerent, Irritable, Argumentative.

Canvas (noun) A strong, rough cloth that is used to make bags, tents, and sails.
▪ My niece sent me a canvas bag from Geneva.
A specially prepared piece of cloth backed or framed as a surface on which a picture can be painted by an artist.
▪ The painter remembered to bring her easel, paints, and brushes, but she forgot a canvas.
(Synonym) Background, Picture, Painting.

Capitulate (verb) To stop fighting an enemy or opponent; to admit that an enemy or opponent has won.
▪ In 1940, the French capitulated to the German invaders.
(Synonym) Surrender, Yield, Succumb. (Antonym) Resist.

Caprice (noun) A sudden change in someone's mood or behavior; usually an unpredictable condition.
▪ We were at the mercy of the manager's every whim and caprice until she was fired.
(Synonym) Notion, Whim, Impulse.

Capture (verb) To take and hold someone as a prisoner, especially by using force.
- The prisoners of war had been captured by enemy soldiers.
(Synonym) Secure, Arrest, Apprehend. (Antonym) Release.

Castigate (verb) To criticize someone harshly.
- He was castigated in the media for a crime he said he did not commit.
(Synonym) Reprimand, Scold, Chastise. (Antonym) Praise.

Catalyst (noun) A person or event that quickly causes change or action.
- Rosa Parks' act of refusing to ride in the back of the bus was the catalyst for the Montgomery bus boycott.
A substance that causes a chemical reaction to happen more quickly.
(Synonym) Facilitator, Vehicle, Promoter.

Catastrophe (noun) A terrible disaster.
- Superstorm Sandy was a terrible catastrophe last summer.
(Synonym) Tragedy, Misfortune, Devastation.

Caucus (noun) A meeting of members of a political party for the purpose of choosing candidates for an election.
- A town caucus will be held for the purpose of nominating candidates.
A group of people united to promote an agreed-upon cause.
(Synonym) Committee, Conference, Meeting.

Cautious (adjective) Careful about avoiding danger or risk.
- Children should be cautious when crossing the street.
(Synonym) Precautious, Discreet, Prudent. (Antonym) Reckless.

Censure (noun) Official strong criticism; the act of blaming or condemning sternly.
- The country faces international censure for its alleged involvement in the assassination.
(Synonym) Criticism, Disapproval, Condemnation. (Antonym) Approval.

Certainty (noun) A fact about which there is no doubt; feeling certain about something.
- There is no certainty about what will happen in the future.
(Synonym) Sureness, Confidence, Assurance.

Chaff (noun) The seed coverings and plant parts that cannot be eaten and are removed from grain; something worthless; waste.
- "Separate the wheat from the chaff" means to distinguish the useful from the useless.

Chagrin (noun) A feeling of being frustrated or annoyed because of failure or disappointment.
- It was a source of chagrin when I could not attend my aunt's funeral.
(Synonym) Humiliation, Annoyance, Embarrassment.

Challenge (verb) To say or show that something may not be true, correct, or legal.
- In her speech, the class valedictorian challenged the notion of mandatory education.
To test the ability, skill, or strength of someone; to be difficult enough; to invite into competition.
- The new software will challenge the children in math.
(Synonym) Contest, Dispute, Oppose.

Chameleon (noun) A type of lizard that can change the color of its skin to blend in with the colors around it; a person who often changes his or her ideas or character in order to please others or to succeed; one who is subject to quick or frequent change, especially in appearance.
- The senator is a political chameleon; he is inconsistent, and he often changes his political beliefs.
(Synonym) Changeable person.

Champion (noun) A winner of first prize or first place in competition; one who shows marked superiority.
- Our baseball team will play the defending champion in the final game on Thursday.
A militant advocate or defender; someone who fights or speaks publicly in support of a person, belief, or cause; to side with.
- Harriet Tubman was a champion of civil rights.
(Synonym) Warrior, Backer, Advocate.

Chaos (noun) Complete confusion and disorder; a state in which behavior and events are not controlled by anything.
- The Haitian earthquake caused chaos throughout the city of Port-au-Prince.
The state of the universe before there was any order and before stars and planets were formed.
(Synonym) Turmoil, Anarchy, Commotion. (Antonym) Order.

Charisma (noun) A special magnetic charm or appeal that causes people to feel attracted and excited by a person, especially a public figure such as a political leader.
- Pope John Paul II's charisma was one factor that made him the most beloved pope of all time.
(Synonym) Captivation, Magnetism, Personality.

Charlatan (noun) A person who pretends to know or be something in order to deceive people.
- Some patients thought he was a great doctor, but others knew he was a charlatan.
(Synonym) Impostor, Fake, Fraud.

Charm (noun) Something that is believed to have magic powers, especially to prevent bad luck and to ensure good fortune.
- I keep my lucky coin as a good-luck charm.
A trait that fascinates, allures, or delights; a physical grace or attraction; an attractive quality.
- He fell under the spell of her charms; she had a magnetic personality.
(Synonym) Attractiveness, Charisma, Keepsake.

Chassis (noun) The supporting frame upon which the main parts of an automobile are built.
▪ The speed bump scraped the chassis of my car.
(Synonym) Skeleton, Frame, Carcass.

Chastise (verb) To criticize someone harshly for doing something wrong; to inflict punishment or to censure severely.
▪ My parents chastised me for forgetting to walk the dog.
(Synonym) Scold, Censure, Punish.

Chauffeur (noun) A person whose job is to drive people around in a car.
▪ Anne's chauffeur picked her up from school and dropped her off at her house every day.

Chide (verb) To reproach in a mild and constructive manner; to scold someone gently; to voice disapproval to.
▪ The teacher chided us for missing school for two consecutive days.
(Synonym) Reprimand, Blame, Rebuke. (Antonym) Praise.

Chilly (adjective) Noticeably cold; unpleasantly affected by cold; Unfriendly.
▪ You must be chilly wearing those short pants in the winter.
(Synonym) Icy, Frosty, Aloof.

Chronic (adjective) Continuing or occurring again and again for a long time, not acute.
▪ She has a chronic disease.
(Synonym) Persistent, Long-lasting, Enduring. (Antonym) Fleeting.

Circuitous (adjective) Indirect; going the long way around; not said or done simply or clearly.
▪ He took a circuitous route to the pharmacy to avoid meeting the thugs.
(Synonym) Indirect, Tortuous, Roundabout. (Antonym) Direct.

Cistern (noun) A container that holds a supply of water; an underground water tank that is used for storing rainwater.
▪ The cistern collected all of the rainwater from the hurricane.

Citadel (noun) A fortress or a castle that in past times was used to protect the city if the city was attacked.
▪ We visited the Acropolis, the most famous citadel in Athens.
(Synonym) Bastion, Stronghold, Refuge.

Clammy (adjective) Being damp, soft, sticky, unpleasantly wet and cold; lacking normal human warmth.
▪ The clammy atmosphere of the school made me sad.
(Synonym) Moist, Humid, Muggy. (Antonym) Dry.

Clamor (noun) A loud continuous noise.
▪ The clamor of the approaching train woke me up in the middle of the night.
Strong demand for something; insistent public expression as in support or protest.

- There is growing clamor for health-care reform.
(Synonym) Uproar, Request, Commotion.

Clandestine (adjective) Done in a private place or way; done secretly.
- The opposition had a clandestine meeting to overthrow the government.
(Synonym) Underground, Illegal, Stealthy.

Coarse (adjective) Made up of large pieces; not fine, having a rough quality.
- The cheap coat was made of a coarse fabric.
Crude or unrefined in taste, manners, or language; rude or offensive; of ordinary or inferior quality or value.
(Synonym) Stiff, Harsh, Common.

Cobble (verb) To make something by putting together different parts in a quick way; to make or repair shoes.
- We bought expensive leather shoes cobbled in Spain.

Coddle (verb) To treat someone with too much care or kindness.
- The mother coddled the toddler in the chilly winter.
(Synonym) Indulge, Overprotect, Baby.

Coerce (verb) To get something by using force or threats.
- The robber coerced the bank clerk to give her the money.
(Synonym) Compel, Intimidate, Persuade.

Collide (verb) To hit something or each other with strong force; to crash.
- He was killed when a truck collided with his car.
(Synonym) Smash together, Bump into, Strike.

Collusion (noun) Secret agreement or cooperation for an illegal or dishonest purpose.
- The company's employees were acting in collusion to steal money.
(Synonym) Conspiracy, Complicity, Connivance.

Colossal (adjective) Very large or great; of an exceptional or astonishing degree.
- They have erected a colossal statue in front of the stadium.
(Synonym) Huge, Gigantic, Enormous. (Antonym) Tiny.

Combative (adjective) Having or showing a willingness to fight or argue.
- The protesters from Ferguson were not combative; they were marching peacefully.
(Synonym) Aggressive, Belligerent, Argumentative. (Antonym) Peaceable.

Commencement (noun) The time when something begins; the ceremonies or the day for conferring degrees or diplomas to students who have graduated from a school or college.
- The former governor spoke at the commencement.
(Synonym) Beginning, Inauguration, Graduation ceremony.

Commend (verb) To praise someone in a serious and often public way; to mention as deserving attention or approval.
- I commend Katie for her poise and grace during her final presentation.
(Synonym) Entrust, Applaud, Acclaim.

Commensurate (adjective) Equal or similar to something in size, amount, or degree.
- The symphony orchestra offered Elizabeth a salary commensurate with her ability as a violinist.
(Synonym) Matching, Corresponding, Proportionate.

Common (adjective) Without special rank or status; not having power, wealth, or high status.
- Under British law, a common person does not have title, rank, or status.
Belonging to or shared by two or more people or groups; occurring or appearing frequently; not rare.
- Nowadays, it is common for children to own an iPod.
(Synonym) Corporate, Usual, Typical.

Commotion (noun) Noisy excitement and confusion; an agitated disturbance.
- There was a sudden commotion when the president and first lady entered the restaurant.
(Synonym) Turmoil, Uproar, Disorder.

Compel (verb) To force someone to do something.
- I am compelled to stay at the hospital because of illness.
To drive or urge forcefully or irresistibly; to cause to do or occur by overwhelming pressure.
(Synonym) Coerce, Require, Oblige.

Competent (adjective) Having the necessary ability or skills; able to do something well or well enough to meet a standard.
- She is competent at fixing electric machinery.
Able to take part in a trial.
- They sent her to a mental institution because she was not competent to stand trial.
(Synonym) Capable, Knowledgeable, Experienced. (Antonym) Inept.

Complimentary (adjective) Expressing praise or admiration for someone.
- Her professor made complimentary remarks about her achievements.
Given for free as a courtesy or favor.
- The New York-Presbyterian Hospital offers valet parking as a complimentary service to patients.
(Synonym) Courtesy, Gratis, Free of charge.

Comprehend (verb) To understand something, such as a difficult or complex subject.
- This math problem is easy to comprehend.
(Synonym) Grasp, Figure out, Understand.

Compress (verb) To reduce in size, quantity, or volume as if by squeezing to fill less space; to reduce the size of a computer file by using special software.
▪ We need to compress the forty-page manual into thirty-five pages.
(Synonym) Constrict, Compact, Condense. (Antonym) Expand.

Compromise (noun) A way of reaching agreement in which each person or group gives up something that was wanted in order to end an argument or dispute.
▪ I am always ready to seek compromise in order to avoid an argument with my friend.
(Synonym) Cooperation, Negotiation, Concession.

Conceal (verb) To hide something or someone from sight; to keep something secret.
▪ The pilot seems to have concealed his illness from his employers.
(Synonym) Cover, Obscure, Disguise. (Antonym) Reveal.

Conciliate (verb) To become friendly or agreeable; to bring into agreement.
▪ Michael is sending flowers in order to conciliate his girlfriend after their fight the night before.
(Synonym) Appeased, Pacify, Make peace. (Antonym) Provoke.

Concise (adjective) Using few words; not including extra or unnecessary information.
▪ Your essay should be clear and concise.
(Synonym) Abridged, Brief, Succinct.

Concur (verb) To agree with someone or something; to act together to a common end or single effect.
▪ We concur that more money should be spent on education.
(Synonym) Be in accord, Coincide, Harmonize. (Antonym) Conflict.

Condone (verb) To forgive or approve something that is considered wrong; to regard or treat something bad or blameworthy as acceptable, forgivable, or harmless.
▪ The mayor has been accused of condoning racism.
(Synonym) Disregard, Tolerate, Overlook.

Confide (verb) To tell something that is secret or private to someone one trusts; to show confidence by imparting secrets.
▪ She confided to me that she is not good at spelling.
(Synonym) Reveal, Entrust, Confess.

Conflict (noun) Strong disagreement between people, groups, ideas, or feelings that results in angry argument.
▪ In parts of Africa, there are conflicts between tribes.
(Synonym) Battle, Quarrel, Divergence.

Congeal (verb) To become thick or solid.
▪ My wound congealed because I did not have immediate care.
(Synonym) Coagulate, Thicken, Harden. (Antonym) Liquefy.

Congenial (adjective) Suitable or appropriate; pleasant and enjoyable; friendly.
- I like being in her company because she is congenial and outgoing.

Having the same nature, disposition, tastes, or outlook.
- This restaurant offers an atmosphere congenial to entertaining.

(Synonym) Suitable, Friendly, Agreeable. (Antonym) Hostile.

Congenital (adjective) Existing since birth; acquired during development in the uterus and not through heredity.
- She suffers from congenital heart disease.

(Synonym) Inborn, Inherent, Natural.

Connivance (noun) To secretly help someone do something dishonest or illegal.
- With the connivance of his assistant, the financial officer stole millions of dollars from the bank.

(Synonym) Involvement, Collusion, Participation.

Connoisseur (noun) An expert in a particular subject; one who understands the details, technique, or principles of a subject; one who enjoys with discrimination and appreciation of subtleties and is competent to act as a critical judge.
- My friend is a connoisseur of fine French wines.

(Synonym) Specialist, Authority, Expert.

Conspicuous (adjective) Very easy to see or notice; attracting attention; obvious to the eye or mind.
- The directions for the blood test were posted in a conspicuous place for patients.

(Synonym) Evident, In the limelight, Visible.

Construct (verb) To make by combining parts or elements to build something physical, such as a road, bridge, or building; to make or create by organizing ideas and words.
- They plan to construct a community pool in the neighborhood.

(Synonym) Build, Erect, Compose.

Contained (verb) To have or include; to keep from spreading.
- The jar contained five dollars in pennies.

(Synonym) Enclosed, Included, Held.

Contaminate (verb) To soil, stain, corrupt, or infect by contact; to make unfit for use, dangerous, dirty, or impure by adding something harmful or undesirable to it.
- We had to buy many bottles of water during our trip because the city water was contaminated with chemicals.

(Synonym) Pollute, Taint, Infect. (Antonym) Purify.

Contemplate (verb) To think deeply or carefully about something; to view or consider with continued attention.
- I need time to contemplate the two job offers before I make a final decision.

(Synonym) Meditate, Ponder, Consider.

Contemporary (adjective) Happening, existing, living, or coming into being during the same period of time; marked by characteristics of the present period.
- Surprisingly, my children do not enjoy contemporary music.
(Synonym) Modern-day, Simultaneous, Current. (Antonym) Old.

Contempt (noun) Not worthy of any respect or approval; lack of respect or reverence for something.
- Myriam looked at the driver with contempt as he made a turn without signaling.
(Synonym) Disdain, Disrespect, Hatred. (Antonym) Admiration.

Contend (verb) To argue or state something in a strong and definite way.
- The defense attorney contended that his client was not competent to stand trial.
To compete with a good chance of winning.
- The basketball team is expected to contend for the championship this year.
To struggle; to deal with something difficult or unpleasant.
- The residents should not have to contend with the crime caused by the construction of additional subways.
(Synonym) Contest, Satisfy, Assert.

Content (verb) To be pleased and satisfied; not needing more.
- The children were content with ice cream and cake for the party.
(Synonym) Gladden, Gratify, Soothe. (Antonym) Unhappy.

Contention (noun) Something such as a belief, opinion, or idea that is argued; stated anger, discord, and disagreement.
- Nowadays, there has been too much contention in the legislative branch of the United States.
(Synonym) Argument, Competition, Controversy. (Antonym) Harmony.

Contest (noun) An event in which people try to win by doing something better than others.
- Chin Yeng won the prize in the final math contest.
(Synonym) Competition, Tournament, Challenge.

Contort (verb) To twist into an unusual appearance or shape.
- John contorted his body to squeeze through the gate of the stadium.
(Synonym) Distort, Bend, Deform.

Contour (noun) The outline or outer edge of something; an outline, especially of a curving or irregular figure.
- The map showed the contour of the coastline.
(Synonym) Curve, Shape, Outline.

Contradiction (noun) The act of saying something that is opposite or very different in meaning to something else.
- The police arrested her because there was a contradiction between the two explanations.
(Synonym) Inconsistency, Paradox, Opposition.

Controversy (noun) Strong disagreement about something among a large group of people; a discussion marked especially by the expression of opposing views.
- There is controversy surrounding abortion rights.
(Synonym) Dispute, Debate, Argument.

Convene (verb) To come together in a group for a meeting.
- The United Nations convened all the heads of state for serious crisis.
(Synonym) Organize, Assemble, Convoke.

Convert (verb) To change from one religion, belief, political party, etc. to another; to change to a different system or method.
- Myriam converted from Protestantism to Catholicism.
(Synonym) Transform, Switch, Renovate.

Convoluted (adjective) Complicated and difficult to understand.
- The book has a convoluted story.
(Synonym) Complex, Tortuous, Twisted. (Antonym) Straightforward.

Copyright (noun) The exclusive legal right to be the only one to reproduce, publish, and sell a book or musical recording for a certain period of time.
- His boss still holds the copyrights to his works.
(Synonym) Patent, Right, Charter.

Corpulent (adjective) Having a fat, large, bulky body; obese.
- The boy has a corpulent body.
(Synonym) Overweight, Obese, Fat. (Antonym) Slim.

Correspondence (noun) The activity of writing letters or e-mails to someone.
- E-mail correspondence has become extremely important for contemporary businesses.
(Synonym) Letter, Communication, Mail.

Corroborate (verb) To support or help prove a statement or theory by providing information or evidence; make more certain.
- The team members corroborated the findings for their science project.
(Synonym) Validate, Confirm, Support. (Antonym) Contradict.

Corrupt (adjective) Doing things that are dishonest or illegal in order to make money or to gain or keep power.
- In some developing countries, the government is incredibly corrupt.
(Synonym) Immoral, Fraudulent, Unethical. (Antonym) Honest.

Counterfeit (verb) To make an exact copy of something in order to trick people; to imitate or feign, especially with intent to deceive.
- They were arrested for counterfeiting money.
(Synonym) Fake, Fabricate, Forge.

Couplet (noun) Two lines of poetry that form a unit.
- He wrote a poem made up of eight couplets.

Crafty (adjective) Clever in usually a deceptive or dishonest way; adept in the use of subtlety and cunning.
- They devised a crafty scheme to defraud the business.
(Synonym) Sneaky, Deceitful, Sly.

Crass (adjective) Having or showing no understanding of what is proper or acceptable; rude and insensitive.
- Her crass comments show that she does not care about the feelings of others.
(Synonym) Ridiculous, Tactless, Thoughtless. (Antonym) Sensitive.

Credible (adjective) Able to be believed; good enough to be effective.
- We need credible information before taking action.
(Synonym) Trustworthy, Sincere, Reliable.

Credulous (adjective) Too ready to believe things; easily fooled or cheated.
- My daughter is not credulous enough to believe such foolishness.
(Synonym) Naïve, Gullible, Innocent.

Criticize (verb) To express disapproval.
- Anne criticized Jane for the heavy makeup she wore to school.
(Synonym) Disparage, Complain, Condemn.

Crone (noun) A cruel or ugly old woman; a withered old woman.
- There is a talk about the old crone who lives alone in her decrepit house.
(Synonym) Witch, Hag, Sorceress.

Crucial (adjective) Extremely important or essential; marked by final determination of a doubtful issue.
- It is crucial for students to maintain a high GPA In order to attend a prestigious university.
(Synonym) Vital, Necessary, Decisive. (Antonym) Trivial.

Crude (adjective) Simple and basic; made or done in a way that does not show a lot of skill.
- After the earthquake, they built small, crude houses out of wood.
Marked by the primitive, gross, or elemental or by uncultivated simplicity or vulgarity.
- The school expelled the boys who were making crude remarks to the young girl.
(Synonym) Rudimentary, Unrefined, Crass.

Crumble (verb) To break into small pieces; to break down completely; to stop functioning.
- I crumbled the bread into tiny pieces.
- Her relationship with her husband is crumbling.
(Synonym) Deteriorate, Fall apart, Collapse.

Culpable (adjective) Deserving blame; guilty of doing something wrong or harmful.
▪ They held him culpable for breaking into the supermarket.
(Synonym) Guilty, Worthy of blame, Responsible.

Culprit (noun) A person who has committed a crime or done something wrong; guilty person; the source or cause of a problem.
▪ The police found the two culprits who had committed the horrible crime.
(Synonym) Offender, Lawbreaker, Criminal.

Cultured (adjective) Having or showing good education, tastes, and manners; grown or made under controlled conditions.
▪ My neighbors are cultured people from the Caribbean Islands.
(Synonym) Well-educated, Cultivated.

Cumbersome (adjective) Hard to handle or manage because of size or weight; complicated and hard to do.
▪ The company's job application process is cumbersome and time-consuming.
Long and difficult to say or read.
▪ I cannot pronounce my daughter-in-law's cumbersome name.
(Synonym) Awkward, Heavy, Burdensome.

Cupidity (noun) A strong desire for money or possessions; inordinate desire for wealth; greed for gain.
▪ Rick's cupidity led him to steal money from the pension funds.
(Synonym) Avarice, Love, Materialism.

Cure (noun) Something such as a drug or medical treatment that stops a disease and makes someone healthy again.
▪ There is recent news that they are close to finding cures for certain types of cancer.
Something that ends a problem or improves a bad situation; a solution.
▪ Exercise is a way to cure certain illnesses.
(Synonym) Treatment, Therapy, Treat.

Curmudgeon (noun) A crusty, ill-tempered person, usually an old man who is easily annoyed or angered and who often complains.
▪ Bernie, the lonely old curmudgeon who lived in our neighborhood, died last week.

Daring (adjective) Willing to do dangerous or difficult things; bold in action or thought; showing a lack of fear; prepared to take risks.
▪ She is a daring mountain climber.
(Synonym) Brave, Intrepid, Courageous.

Dearth (noun) The state or condition of not having enough of something; an inadequate supply; lack of.
▪ The dearth of affordable housing in the city forced many families to leave the area.
(Synonym) Scarcity, Shortage, Deficiency.

QUIZ # 3- MATCH EACH WORD IN THE FIRST COLUMN WITH ITS SYNONYM IN THE SECOND COLUMN. CHECK YOUR ANSWERS IN THE BACK OF THE BOOK.

1. cacophony	a. false
2. camouflage	b. noise
3. candid	c. force
4. citadel	d. love
5. clamor	e. honest
6. colossal	f. dissonance
7. compel	g. gigantic
8. concise	h. inborn
9. condone	i. letter
10. congenital	j. approve
11. controversy	k. confirm
12. correspondence	l. disguise
13. corroborate	m. fort
14. counterfeit	n. brief
15. cupidity	o. debate

Debris (noun) The junk pieces or remains that are left after something has been broken down or destroyed.
▪ After Haiti's 2010 earthquake, many people began digging through the debris in search of survivors.
(Synonym) Wreckage, Rubble, Waste.

Debunk (verb) To show that something such as a belief or theory is not true; to show the falseness of a story, idea, statement, etc.
▪ Long ago, scientists debunked the idea that the Earth was flat.
(Synonym) Expose, Demystify, Discredit.

Deceit (noun) The quality of being dishonest.
▪ He became wealthy through lies and deceit.
(Synonym) Deception, Trick, Fraud.

Deceive (verb) To cause to believe what is not true; mislead; to fail to fulfill.
▪ Appearances can be deceiving.
(Synonym) Betray, Misinform, Trick.

Deception (noun) The act of making someone believe something that is not true; the act of deceiving someone.
▪ Many did not know of Judas's deception until it was too late.
(Synonym) Trickery, Deceit, Ruse. (Antonym) Truthfulness.

Decimate (verb) To severely damage or destroy a large part of; to cause great destruction or harm to.
▪ The forest has been decimated by air pollution.
(Synonym) Annihilate, Ruin, Demolish.

Decline (verb) To become lower in amount or less in number; to say that you will not or cannot do something; to tend toward an inferior state or weaker condition; to slope downward.
▪ Oil prices continue to decline.
(Synonym) Reject, Decrease, Refuse. (Antonym) Accept.

Decomposition (noun) The process of being slowly destroyed and broken down by natural processes or chemicals.
▪ Bacteria and fungi help in the decomposition of organic matter.
(Synonym) Decay, Putrefaction, Disintegration.

Decorum (noun) Polite behavior that shows good taste in conduct or appearance; respect and good manners.
▪ The royal family placed a high value on honor, decorum, and respectability.
(Synonym) Etiquette, Gentility, Good manners.

Deduct (verb) To take away something, especially an amount of money from a total.
▪ The price of the spoiled food that I received from the supermarket was deducted from my final payment.
(Synonym) Remove, Decrease by, Subtract.

Deftly (adverb) Characterized by facility, skill, and cleverness; able to do something quickly and accurately.
▪ The rapper is known for deftly rhyming words.
(Synonym) Adeptly, Skillfully, Neatly. (Antonym) Clumsily.

Dehydrate (verb) To lose water or body fluids.
▪ Athletes need to drink lots of water in order to not dehydrate.
(Synonym) Dry out, Parch, Desiccate.

Dejected (adjective) Sad because of failure, loss; cast down in spirits.
▪ She has been deeply dejected since her husband abandoned her.
(Synonym) Disappointed, Miserable, Unhappy. (Antonym) Cheerful.

Delay (noun) A situation in which something happens later than it should.
▪ After months of delay, they have finally opened the new hospital in our community.
(Synonym) Postponement, Interruption, Adjournment.

Delectable (adjective) Very pleasant to taste or smell; delicious. very attractive; highly pleasing; delightful.

- My children surprised me for my birthday with delicious foods and an array of delectable desserts.

(Synonym) Delicious, Enjoyable, Charming.

Deliberate (adjective) Done or said in a way that is planned or intended; done or said on purpose.
- The jury found out that the killing was deliberate. Thus, it was not an accidental death.

(Synonym) Thoughtful, Premeditated, Intentional. (Antonym) Accidental.

Delicate (adjective) Easily broken or damaged; not robust in health or constitution.
- The vase is quite delicate, so please handle with care.

(Synonym) Subtle, Soft, Fragile.

Delinquent (noun) A young person who regularly does illegal or immoral things.
- The juvenile delinquent was in court for shoplifting.

(Synonym) Negligent, Offending, Criminal.

Dell (noun) A small valley with trees and grass growing in it.
- The wooded dell contained many hallowed trees.

Deluge (noun) A situation in which a large area of land becomes completely covered with water; flood; a drenching rain.
- In the Bible, the deluge killed everyone except Noah and his family.

(Synonym) Inundation, Overflow, Overwhelm.

Demagogue (noun) A political leader who tries to get support by making false claims and promises and by using arguments based on emotion rather than reason.
- The presidential candidate is a bigoted demagogue.

(Synonym) Agitator, Manipulator.

Demeanor (noun) A person's appearance and behavior; outward manner or behavior.
- She has a quiet demeanor.

(Synonym) Conduct, Manner, Deportment.

Demonstrate (verb) To explain or prove by use of examples or experiments.
- Applicants for the accounting jobs must demonstrate strong knowledge of Excel and QuickBooks.

To take part in a public display in order to show support or oppose something.
- Protesters demonstrated after the not-guilty verdict was announced.

(Synonym) Exhibit, Reveal, Show.

Depict (verb) To represent in a picture, sculpture, painting, photograph.
- The book depicts the story of the unsung heroes of the civil rights movement.

(Synonym) Describe, Portray, Illustrate.

Deplete (verb) To use most or all of; to greatly reduce in amount by using up; to empty.

- A shocking study found that ocean life and seafood could be depleted by as early as 2048. (Synonym) Lessen, Diminish, Exhaust. (Antonym) Increase.

Deplore (verb) To feel or express grief for; to strongly disapprove.
- We deplore the passing of our beloved teacher.
(Synonym) Condemn, Lament, Regret.

Deport (verb) To force a person who is not a citizen to leave a country.
- The Department of Homeland Security deported thousands of undocumented immigrants last year.
(Synonym) Expatriate, Extradite, Banish.

Depth (noun) A distance below a surface.
- The swimming pool in the school gymnasium has a maximum depth of seven feet.
(Synonym) Penetration, Profundity, Complexity.

Desecrate (verb) To damage a holy place or object; to treat a holy place or object with disrespect; profane.
- The vandals were accused of desecrating the church altar.
(Synonym) Blaspheme, Defile, Vandalize.

Desiccated (adjective) Having had the water removed; to dry up; to preserve a food by drying; very dry.
- Raisins are desiccated grapes.
(Synonym) Dehydrated, Parched, Shriveled. (Antonym) Moist.

Desperado (noun) A bold or violent criminal who is not afraid of getting hurt or caught.
- The notorious desperados of the Old West robbed banks, stagecoaches, and trains.
(Synonym) Bandit, Villain, Outlaw.

Desperate (adjective) Very sad and upset because of having little or no hope; feeling or showing despair.
- She became desperate after losing her job.
(Synonym) Anxious, Frantic, Worried. (Antonym) Calm.

Despondent (adjective) Very sad and without hope; feeling or showing extreme discouragement, dejection, or depression.
- She was despondent over the loss of her house.
(Synonym) Hopeless, Pessimistic, Miserable. (Antonym) Cheerful.

Destroy (verb) To put an end to; to damage something so badly that it cannot be repaired.
- The virus infected the computer and destroyed all the files.
(Synonym) Annihilate, Demolish, Subvert.

Detect (verb) To discover the existence of something that is hidden or hard to see or hear.
- It is crucial to place devices in your home to detect fire, smoke, and carbon monoxide.

(Synonym) Notice, Identify, Spot.

Deter (verb) To cause someone to decide not to do something; to prevent something from happening; to discourage.
- My father bought a huge dog to deter burglars.
(Synonym) Daunt, Dissuade, Hinder. (Antonym) Encourage.

Detriment (noun) A cause of loss, injury, or damage.
- She invested all her time into her accounting career, to the detriment of her children.
(Synonym) Impairment, Harm, Disadvantage. (Antonym) Benefit.

Devise (verb) To invent or plan something that is difficult or complicated; to think up.
- Scientists are devising a plan to help Alzheimer's patients.
(Synonym) Formulate, Develop, Create.

Dexterity (noun) The ability to use one's hands skillfully; readiness and grace in physical activity; the ability to think and act quickly and cleverly; adroitness.
- I love going to the circus to revel at the amazing dexterity of the acrobats.
(Synonym) Deftness, Nimbleness, Agility. (Antonym) Clumsiness.

Dialogue (noun) A conversation between two or more people; an exchange of ideas and opinions.
- Elizabeth and I had a lengthy dialogue about her plans for college.
(Synonym) Talk, Discussion, Exchange of ideas.

Diffidence (noun) A lack of confidence; a state of not feeling comfortable around people.
- He exhibited diffidence around people he did not know.
(Synonym) Reserve, Shyness, Reticence.

Dignify (verb) To give dignity or importance to something.
- The presence of the first lady at your high school graduation will dignify the ceremony.
(Synonym) Exalt, Distinguish, Honor. (Antonym) Degrade.

Dilate (verb) To become larger or wider; to enlarge or expand in bulk or extent.
- The medicine causes the blood vessels *to* dilate.
(Synonym) Amplify, Elaborate, Enlarge.

Diligent (adjective) Careful hard work; continued energetic effort.
- My dad is a diligent worker.
(Synonym) Persistent, Industrious, Meticulous. (Antonym) Lazy.

Dim (adjective) Not bright or clear; having a limited or insufficient amount of light; not likely to be good or successful.
- We were sitting in a dim corner of the restaurant.
(Synonym) Dull, Blurry, Unclear.

Diminution (noun) The act or process of becoming less.
▪ There has been a diminution of my income over the past three years.
(Synonym) Decrease, Dwindling, Reduction. (Antonym) Growth.

Diminutive (adjective) Very small; exceptionally or notably small.
▪ My French teacher is diminutive yet imposing.
(Synonym) Tiny, Miniature, Minuscule.

Din (noun) Loud, continuous noise.
▪ It was hard to hear my friends over the din in the school cafeteria.
(Synonym) Commotion, Clamor, Tumult.

Discard (verb) To throw something away because it is useless or unwanted; to remove a playing card from your hand in a card game.
▪ I want to discard the clothes that I have not worn recently and send them to charity.
(Synonym) Dispose of, Get rid of, Reject. (Antonym) Keep.

Disclose (verb) To make something known to the public; to open up.
▪ If you want to run for office, you have to disclose the sources of your income.
(Synonym) Divulge, Reveal, Make known. (Antonym) Conceal.

Disdain (noun) A feeling of strong dislike or disapproval of.
▪ When the man leered at her, she looked back at him with disdain.
(Synonym) Scorn, Contempt, Spurn. (Antonym) Respect.

Disguise (verb) To change the usual appearance, sound, taste of; to prevent recognition; false front.
▪ He tried to disguise himself, but the police recognized and caught him anyway.
(Synonym) Camouflage, Conceal, Hide. (Antonym) Reveal.

Dismal (adjective) Lacking merit; particularly very bad or poor; showing or causing unhappiness or sad feelings, not warm; causing gloom or depression.
▪ The weather looks dismal today; thus, I will stay indoors.
(Synonym) Disastrous, Dreadful, Bleak.

Dismantle (verb) To tear down or take apart.
▪ The computer engineer dismantled the computer in order to repair it.
(Synonym) Demolish, Break down, Pull apart. (Antonym) Assemble.

Dismay (verb) To cause someone to feel very worried, disappointed, or upset.
▪ Our grandfather always advised us to not let ourselves be dismayed by the task before us.
(Synonym) Discourage, Sadden, Depress. (Antonym) Comfort.

Dismiss (verb) To officially end or stop something, such as a legal case.
▪ When Elena went to court to support her son, the judge dismissed all the charges for lack of evidence.

To cause to leave; to remove from position or service.
(Synonym) Discharge, Terminate, Reject. (Antonym) Detain.

Dispatch (verb) To send off to a particular destination with promptness or speed.
▪ The school dispatched a taxi to pick us up from the airport.
(Synonym) Transmit, Send out, Forward.

Dispensary (noun) A place where medicine or minor medical treatment is given; an infirmary.
▪ I had the cut dressed at the hospital dispensary.

Disseminate (verb) To cause something, such as information, to go to many people; to spread abroad as though sowing seed; to disperse throughout.
▪ The spread of Internet allows us to disseminate information faster.
(Synonym) Distribute, Broadcast, Propagate.

Dissident (noun) Someone who strongly and publicly disagrees with and criticizes the government.
▪ The headmaster called the parents of all student dissidents for a serious meeting.
(Synonym) Protestor, Revolutionist, Rebellious. (Antonym) Conformist.

Distraught (adjective) Very upset; so upset that you are not able to think clearly or behave normally; agitated with doubt or mental conflict or pain; mentally deranged.
▪ She was so distraught over the death of her husband that she could not eat or sleep.
(Synonym) Distressed, Hysterical, Disturbed. (Antonym) Calm.

Diverge (verb) To split and move out in different directions from a single point; change course.
▪ After high school, all of her friends diverged to attend college in different states.
(Synonym) Move away, Deviate, Separate. (Antonym) Converge.

Diversity (noun) Having people who are of different races or different cultures in a group or organization.
▪ The city of New York is known for its cultural diversity.
(Synonym) Variety, Assortment, Mixture.

Divert (verb) To turn from one course or use to another; to turn aside; to change the direction.
▪ Police diverted traffic to a side street due to an accident.
To take the attention away.
▪ He feigned a stomachache to divert his mom's attention from his bad grades.
To entertain; to amuse.
(Synonym) Deviate, Distract, Recreate.

Divisive (adjective) Causing disagreement between people and causing them to separate into different groups.

▪ We need to avoid discussing divisive topics or our meetings will go on for hours. (Synonym) Discordant, Factious, Troublesome. (Antonym) Unified.

Divulge (verb) To reveal or make known; disclose.
▪ A gossip columnist's job is to divulge information about celebrities.
(Synonym) Reveal, Tell, Disclose.

Docile (adjective) Easily taught, trained, controlled, or managed.
▪ My dog is docile and easy to handle.
(Synonym) Passive, Tame, Submissive.

Dogmatic (adjective) Expressing personal opinions or beliefs as if they are certainly correct and cannot be doubted.
▪ He became so dogmatic that you cannot prevail when arguing with him.
(Synonym) Rigid, Strict, Opinionated. (Antonym) Flexible.

Domicile (noun) A person's fixed, permanent, and principal home.
▪ Students must establish a domicile in the state to be eligible for reduced tuition.
(Synonym) Dwelling, Abode, Residence.

Donor (noun) A person or group who gives, donates, or contributes in order to help a person or organization.
▪ The family is one of the private school's major donors.
(Synonym) Supporter, Patron, Contributor.

Dormant (adjective) Not doing anything at this time; not active; marked by a suspension of activity.
▪ The business has been dormant since the economic downturn.
(Synonym) Asleep, Inactive, Sluggish.

Douse (verb) To plunge into liquid; immerse; to extinguish a fire with water.
▪ It took firefighters an entire day to douse the blaze in the woods.
(Synonym) Drench, Extinguish, Soak.

Dowdy (adjective) Having a dull or uninteresting appearance; not attractive or stylish.
▪ Jinette played a dowdy old woman in the film.
(Synonym) Old-fashioned, Plain, Shabby. (Antonym) Chic.

Doze (verb) To sleep lightly especially for a short period of time; to be in a dull or stupefied condition.
▪ A few students dozed off during Latin class.
(Synonym) Take a nap, Slumber, Sleep.

Dread (verb) To be in great fear.
▪ I won't play in the basement because I dread being in dark, dank places.
(Synonym) Be Terrified of.

Dreary (adjective) Causing unhappiness or sad feelings; not warm or cheerful.
- She longed to leave her dreary suburb.
(Synonym) Gloomy, Dismal, Lifeless.

Drench (verb) To make completely wet.
- We arrived at the party completely drenched from the unexpected rainstorm.
(Synonym) Saturate, Soak, Inundate.

Drivel (noun) Foolish writing or speech; silly nonsense.
- Don't waste your time listening to this drivel.
(Synonym) Twaddle, Rubbish, Idiocy. (Antonym) Sense.

Dubious (adjective) Unsure or uncertain; feeling doubt about something; likely to be bad or wrong.
- I did not invest a lot of money in this project because I was dubious about our chances for success.
(Synonym) Hesitant, Questioning, Suspicious. (Antonym) Certain.

Duplicate (noun) Made as an exact copy of something else; being the same as another.
- I keep a duplicate of my driver's license in my car.
(Synonym) Photocopy, Reproduction, Replacement.

Duration (noun) The length of time that something exists or lasts; until the end of something.
- The camera remained on the artist for the duration of the concert.
(Synonym) Extent, Period, Term.

Dwindle (verb) To gradually become smaller; to become steadily less.
- If you do not manage it properly, your wealth will dwindle away.
(Synonym) Decrease, Shrink, Reduce.

Ebb (noun) A point reached after things has gotten worse.
- His grades in college reached their lowest ebb after his illness.

Ebb (verb) To flow outward from the land; ; the flowing out of the tide; to get worse.
- She advised her daughter to wait for the tide to ebb before swimming in the bay.
(Synonym) Outgoing tide, Decline, Wane. (Antonym) Flow.

Eclipse (noun) The cutting off of some or all of the light from one celestial body by another.
- The day darkened at the time of the solar eclipse.
A loss of power, success, popularity; the state of being eclipsed.
- Computers led to the eclipse of typewriter.
(Synonym) Break, interruption, Occultation.

QUIZ 4- MATCH EACH WORD IN THE FIRST COLUMN WITH ITS SYNONYM IN THE SECOND COLUMN. CHECK YOUR ANSWERS IN THE BACK OF THE BOOK.

1. dearth	a. rebellious
2. debunk	b. banish
3. deplete	c. discredit
4. deplore	d. shrink
5. deport	e. shortage
6. deter	f. industrious
7. detriment	g. opinionated
8. dialogue	h. discourage
9. diligent	i. reduce
10. diminution	j. conversation
11. dissident	k. reduction
12. diversity	l. inactive
13. dogmatic	m. variety
14. dormant	n. harmful
15. dwindle	o. lament

Ecology (noun) A science that deals with the relationships between groups of living things and their environments.
▪ My counselor advised me to study marine ecology.
(Synonym) Environmental science, Ecosystem.

Ecstasy (noun) A state of very great happiness; extreme delight; being beyond reason and self-control.
▪ The breeze off the river sent me into ecstasies that inspired me to write.
(Synonym) Frenzy, Elation, Excitement.

Edible (adjective) Suitable or safe to eat; eatable.
▪ The decorations look like flowers, but they are edible arrangements of fruit.
(Synonym) Comestible, Palatable, Appetizing.

Eerie (adjective) Strange and mysterious; affected with fright; scared; causing fear.
▪ The thunderstorm created an eerie light.
(Synonym) Sinister, Alarming, Creepy.

Effective (adjective) Producing a result that is wanted; having an intended effect; starting at a particular time.
▪ The 3 percent raise will become effective next month.
(Synonym) Active, Current, In effect.

Efficient (adjective) Capable of producing desired results without wasting materials, time, or energy.
- As a worker, you should be efficient and effective.
(Synonym) Competent, Effective, Resourceful.

Egress (noun) A way to get out of a place or the act of leaving a place; exit.
- The airplane is designed to provide easy egress in case of an emergency.
(Synonym) Door, Way out, Exit. (Antonym) Entrance.

Elaborate (adjective) Made or done with great care or with much detail; having many parts that are carefully arranged or planned.
- My sister-in-law made elaborate preparations in the house for the newborn child.
(Synonym) Extravagant, Sumptuous, Elegant.

Elegant (adjective) Showing good taste; graceful and attractive; of a high grade or quality.
- He is an elegant rich man.
(Synonym) Stylish, Graceful, Chic.

Elegy (noun) A sad poem or song that expresses sorrow or lamentation for someone who is dead.
- When the choir sang the elegy at my friend's funeral, we were all in tears.
(Synonym) Requiem, Speech, Funeral song.

Elite (noun) The people who have the most wealth and status in a society; a successful and powerful person; the best of a class.
- She boasted that she belongs to the elite class.
(Synonym) Selected, Exclusive, Privileged.

Eloquent (adjective) Having the ability to use language clearly and effectively; marked by forceful and fluent expression.
- Sebastien is an articulate and eloquent speaker.
(Synonym) Expressive, Fluent, Articulate.

Elucidate (verb) To give a clarifying explanation; to make something easy to understand.
- The chief financial officer wants us to elucidate on our decision to fire the bookkeeper.
(Synonym) Explain, Make clear, Clarify. (Antonym) Confuse.

Elusive (adjective) Hard to find or capture; hard to understand, define, or remember.
- It may prove elusive to find a solution to this problem.
(Synonym) Intangible, Hard to get hold of, Slippery.

Emaciated (adjective) To become abnormally thin because of hunger or disease.
- His time spent in jail left him in an emaciated condition.
(Synonym) Skinny, Wasted, Shrunken.

Embody (verb) To represent something in a clear and obvious way; to be a symbol or example of something.
▪ The school embodies its mission to cultivate and educate future global leaders.
(Synonym) Symbolize, Personify, Stand for.

Eminent (adjective) Successful, well known, and respected; prominent.
▪ Ernest Hemingway was an eminent writer.
(Synonym) Outstanding, Distinguished, Reputed. (Antonym) Unknown.

Empathy (noun) The feeling that you understand and share another person's experiences and emotions.
▪ The nurse showed great empathy toward the mentally ill.
(Synonym) Sympathy, Compassion, Understanding. (Antonym) Indifference.

Emphatic (adjective) Said or done in a forceful or definite way.
▪ His emphatic answer was believed by everyone who heard him speak.
(Synonym) Vigorous, Insistent, Ardent. (Antonym) Hesitant.

Employ (verb) To provide someone with a job that pays wages or a salary; to make use of.
▪ She has been employed as a computer engineer for Dell.
(Synonym) Hire, Devote, Utilize. (Antonym) Waste.

Emulate (verb) To try to be like someone you admire; to strive to equal or excel; to imitate by means of an emulator.
▪ I grew up emulating my aunt, who was the best seamstress in the town.
(Synonym) Mimic, Copy, Follow.

Encourage (verb) To make someone more determined, hopeful, or confident; to inspire with courage, spirit, or hope.
▪ Researchers are encouraged by the findings of a cure for cancer.
(Synonym) Reassure, Support, Foster.

Endeavor (verb) To make an effort; to seriously or continually try hard; to strive to achieve.
▪ The school endeavors to teach students to be good leaders.
(Synonym) Undertake, Attempt, Struggle.

Endorse (verb) To publicly or officially say that you support something; to approve openly.
▪ This shirt is very expensive and is endorsed by several football stars.
To write your name on the back of a check.
▪ Remember to endorse the check before you deposit it in the ATM.
(Synonym) Favor, Ratify, Authorize. (Antonym) Reject.

Endow (verb) To provide with money for support.
▪ The money will be used to endow the school in perpetuity.
(Synonym) Bequeath, Grant, Donate.

Endure (verb) To continue to exist in the same state or condition.
▪ She works hard to make sure her legacy will endure.
To remain firm under suffering or misfortune without yielding.
▪ He endured five years as a prisoner for a crime he did not commit.
(Synonym) Tolerate, Sustain, Stick with.

Engaged (adjective) Promised to be married.
▪ The engaged man and women plan to honeymoon in Kenya.

Engaged (verb) To hire someone to perform a particular service.
▪ He engaged the services of a plumber when the pipe under the sink broke.
(Synonym) Employed, Involved, Occupied.

Enhance (verb) To increase or improve something in value, quality, or attractiveness.
▪ She sells a facial cream with promises that it will enhance beauty.
(Synonym) Improve, Boost, Enrich.

Enigma (noun) Something that is difficult to understand or explain.
▪ The disappearance of the leader is one of the great enigmas of our time.
(Synonym) Paradox, Puzzle, Mystery.

Enigmatic (adjective) Full of mystery and difficult to understand; mysterious.
▪ Your response is enigmatic.
(Synonym) Inexplicable, Puzzling, Perplexing. (Antonym) Straightforward.

Enlighten (verb) To give knowledge or understanding to someone; to give spiritual insight to.
▪ Can you please enlighten me on this particular issue?
(Synonym) Instruct, Educate, Make clear to.

Enormous (adjective) Marked by extraordinarily great size, number, or degree; exceeding usual bounds or accepted notions.
▪ Elephants are enormous animals.
(Synonym) Huge, Mammoth, Colossal. (Antonym) Tiny.

Enthrall (verb) To hold the attention of someone by being very exciting, interesting, or beautiful.
▪ *The Lion King* on Broadway has enthralled audiences with wonderful songs and beautiful costumes.
(Synonym) Charm, Mesmerize, Captivate. (Antonym) Bore.

Enthusiasm (noun) Strong excitement about something that you like or enjoy.
▪ Alex is doing his work with great energy and enthusiasm.
(Synonym) Eagerness, Passion, Interest. (Antonym) Apathy.

Entice (verb) To attract someone, especially by offering or showing something that is appealing or interesting.
▪ The peddlers hope to entice the children with glittering, illuminated toys.
(Synonym) Cajole, Lure, Tempt.

Entitle (verb) To give a title to something, such as a book.
▪ The president entitled his book *Dreams from My Father*.
To furnish with proper grounds for seeking or claiming something; to give a right to someone.
▪ I am entitled to a great vacation after working so hard during the academic year.
(Synonym) Name, Make eligible, Authorize.

Entourage (noun) A group of people who assist an important person.
▪ The first lady and her entourage entered the hall.
(Synonym) Support, Staff.

Entrepreneur (adjective) A person who starts a business and is willing to risk loss in order to make money.
▪ My cousin is an entrepreneur who started her own computer company after graduating from college.
(Synonym) Businessperson, Industrialist, Magnate.

Entrust (verb) To give someone the responsibility of doing something; to commit to another with confidence.
▪ Maria was entrusted with the responsibility of planning the wedding.
(Synonym) Trust, Delegate, Assign. (Antonym) Deprive.

Envy (noun) The feeling of wanting to have what someone else has.
▪ Her company success made her the envy of her friends.
(Synonym) Resentment, Jealousy, Bitterness. (Antonym) Goodwill.

Ephemeral (adjective) Lasting a very short time; short-lived.
▪ Her unemployment status turned out to be ephemeral; she found work soon after she was fired.
(Synonym) Passing, Temporary, Brief. (Antonym) Permanent.

Equable (adjective) Tending to remain calm; free from sudden or harsh changes.
▪ John displays an equable temperament.
(Synonym) Composed, Serene, Easygoing. (Antonym) Jumpy.

Equine (adjective) Of, relating to, or typical to horses; resembling a horse.
▪ This year, I received a box of equine accessories.
(Synonym) Horsey, Equestrian.

Equitable (adjective) Just or fair; dealing fairly and equally with all concerned.
▪ We fought for more equitable wages among workers.
(Synonym) Reasonable, Unbiased, Fair. (Antonym) Unfair.

Equivocal (adjective) Having two or more possible meanings and usually used to mislead or confuse; ambiguous.
▪ After his lecture, the economist's responses to the students' questions were equivocal.
(Synonym) Vague, Ambivalent, Evasive. (Antonym) Clear.

Era (noun) A period of time that is associated with a particular quality, event, or person; a period identified by some prominent figure or characteristic feature.
▪ The death of Johann Sebastian Bach in 1750 marks the end of the baroque period.
(Synonym) Epoch, Time, Age.

Erect (verb) To raise upward.
▪ They have erected a colossal statue in front of the university.
(Synonym) Establish, Construct, Set up. (Antonym) Dismantle.

Err (verb) To make a mistake; do wrong; sin.
▪ "To err is human" means it is normal for people to make mistakes.
(Synonym) Lapse, Fall, Commit a blunder.

Erratic (adjective) Moving, or changing in ways that are not expected or usual; not consistent or regular; having no fixed course.
▪ His behavior seemed erratic.
(Synonym) Inconsistent, Variable, Unpredictable. (Antonym) Consistent.

Erudite (adjective) knowledge that is deeply learned by studying; scholarly.
▪ She is an erudite scholar.
(Synonym) Knowledgeable, Learned, Studious. (Antonym) Uneducated.

Escalate (verb) To become worse or more severe; to become greater or higher.
▪ I need to receive the invoices in order to escalate payment.
(Synonym) Accelerate, Intensify, Shoot upward.

Esoteric (adjective) Taught to or understood only by members of a special group; limited to a small number of people.
▪ Esoteric religious sects are numerous in his country.
(Synonym) Obscure, Secret, Mysterious.

Essential (adjective) Extremely important and necessary; of the utmost importance, fundamental.
▪ Freedom of speech is an essential right of citizenship.
(Synonym) Indispensable, Vital, Necessary.

Etch (verb) To produce a pattern or design by using a tool or acid to cut the surface of metal or glass; to delineate or impress clearly.
▪ I etched my name on the back of my lucky charm.
(Synonym) Carve, Sketch, Engrave.

Etiquette (noun) The rules indicating the proper and polite way to behave.
▪ You should pay attention to etiquette when you have been invited to a formal occasion.
(Synonym) Protocol, Decorum, Manners.

Étude (noun) A piece of music for the practice of a point of technique; a composition built on a technical motive but played for its artistic value.
▪ Chopin's set of études are the most technically difficult pieces in the solo piano repertoire.

Eulogy (noun) A speech that praises someone who has died.
▪ We were in tears when he delivered a moving eulogy at his father's funeral.
(Synonym) Homage, Praise, Tribute.

Euphoria (noun) Feeling of great happiness and excitement; a feeling of well-being or elation.
▪ Euphoria swept over us when our son passed the bar exam.
(Synonym) Ecstasy, Joy, Exultation. (Antonym) Despair.

Evade (verb) To stay away; to take refuge in escape or avoidance.
▪ The criminals have managed to evade the police.
(Synonym) Avoid, Elude, Sidestep.

Evasion (noun) The act of avoiding something that you do not want to do or deal with.
▪ He was jailed for tax evasion.
(Synonym) Elusion, Dodging, Circumvention.

Evasive (adjective) Not honest or direct; done to avoid harm or an accident.
▪ You are being evasive to avoid telling the truth.
(Synonym) Elusive, Equivocal, Ambiguous. (Antonym) Direct.

Evidence (noun) Something that furnishes proof; material that is presented in a court of law to help find the truth of a matter.
▪ The new evidence will exonerate my neighbor of criminal charges.
(Synonym) Proof, Testimony, Indication.

Exalt (verb) To raise high in rank, power, or character; to elevate by praise or in estimation.
▪ The president exalted the major general to a place on the Joint Chiefs of Staff.
(Synonym) Acclaim, Promote, Elevate.

Exceed (verb) To be greater, better, or more than; to go beyond the limit.
▪ His performance exceeds expectations.
(Synonym) Surpass, Beat, Go over.

Excess (noun) An amount that is more than the usual or necessary amount.
▪ The blood test shows an excess of sugar in my bloodstream.
(Synonym) Overabundance, Surplus, Extra.

Exemption (noun) Freedom from being required to do something that others are required to do; a source or amount of income that is not taxed.
- They were granted an exemption from working on weekends because of their religious beliefs.

(Synonym) Exception, Immunity, Freedom. (Antonym) Obligation, Inclusion.

Exhaust (verb) To use all of someone's mental or physical energy; to tire out or wear out.
- I am exhausted from doing all the household chores.

To completely use up.
- I have exhausted all my savings for a trip to Cambodia.

(Synonym) Drain, Deplete, Fatigue. (Antonym) Refresh.

Exhibit (verb) To make a painting or sculpture available for people to see; to show or reveal.
- Next week, they will exhibit the Renaissance tapestry at the Metropolitan Museum of Art in New York.

(Synonym) Unveil, Demonstrate, Display.

Exhilarated (verb) To cause someone to feel very happy and excited; cheerful.
- We were exhilarated by the news of her nomination for the achievement award.

(Synonym) Overjoyed, Delighted, Energized.

Exhume (verb) To remove a body from the place where it is buried.
- The family exhumed my uncle's body to send him to his home country.

(Synonym) Unearth, Dig up, Disinter. (Antonym) Bury.

Exonerate (verb) To relieve of a responsibility, obligation, or hardship; to clear from accusation or blame.
- The new evidence will exonerate my neighbor of criminal charges.

(Synonym) Forgive, Absolve, Acquit. (Antonym) Blamed.

Exorbitant (adjective) Going far beyond what is fair, very expensive; immoderate.
- They were charged an exorbitant price for replacing the carpet.

(Synonym) Unreasonable, Outrageous, Excessive.

Exotic (adjective) Very different, strange, or unusual; introduced from another country.
- My mother has exotic tastes.

(Synonym) Interesting, Exceptional, Bizarre. (Antonym) Ordinary.

Expedient (adjective) Providing an easy and quick way to solve a problem; a means to an end.
- I found it more expedient to take the train instead of the bus to work today.

(Synonym) Practical, Convenient, Efficient.

Expedite (verb) To cause something to happen faster; to accelerate the process; speed up.
- We will do what we can to expedite payment of the invoices.

(Synonym) Advance, Hurry up, Hasten. (Antonym) Impede.

Expel (verb) To officially force someone to leave a place or organization; to push or force out.
▪ He was expelled from the school for his extreme stance on terrorism.
(Synonym) Banish, Eject, Cast out.

Explicit (adjective) Very clear and complete; leaving no doubt about the meaning or intent.
▪ The teacher gave the class explicit instructions on how to get the assignment done.
(Synonym) Obvious, Clearly stated, Open. (Antonym) Implicit.

Expunged (verb) To efface completely; destroy.
▪ The misdemeanor charges were expunged from his record.
(Synonym) Purged, Removed, Erased.

QUIZ 5.- MATCH EACH WORD IN THE FIRST COLUMN WITH ITS SYNONYM IN THE SECOND COLUMN. CHECK YOUR ANSWERS IN THE BACK OF THE BOOK.

1. eerie	a. surplus
2. egress	b. mystery
3. elucidate	c. strange
4. emulate	d. excessive
5. enigma	e. knowledgeable
6. envy	f. make clear
7. erratic	g. erase
8. erudite	h. elevate
9. etch	i. hasten
10. exalt	j. tired
11. excess	k. exit
12. exhaust	l. inconsistent
13. exorbitant	m. imitate
14. expedite	n. engrave
15. expunged	o. jealousy

Extend (verb) To stretch to full length; unbend.
▪ The tennis table measures nine feet long and five feet wide when it is fully extended.
(Synonym) Range, Encompass, Spread.

Extenuating (adjective) To minimize the seriousness of by making partial excuses.
▪ Due to the death in his family and other extenuating circumstances, the teacher forgave him for not completing his homework.
(Synonym) Explanatory, Mitigating, Justifying.

Extrovert (noun) A friendly person who likes being with and talking to other people; an outgoing person.
- Michael is the most extrovert person I have ever met.

(Synonym) Socializer, Gregarious person, Befriender. (Antonym) Introverted.

Exuberant (adjective) Very lively, happy, or energetic; existing in large amounts; plentiful, abundant.
- George's exuberant personality makes him fun to be around.

(Synonym) Cheerful, Enthusiastic, High-spirited. (Antonym) Lethargic.

Fabricate (verb) To make or build something; to construct, manufacture; to create, invent, or make up something, such as a story in order to trick people.
- He fabricated the storyline for his autobiography.

(Synonym) Put together, Counterfeit, Falsify.

Facet (noun) A part or element of something; an aspect, phase; one of the flat surfaces cut on a gemstone.
- Before choosing a school, you should consider every facet of your decision.

(Synonym) Facade, Component, Side.

Facile (adjective) Too simple; not showing enough thought or effort; easily accomplished or attained.
- If you have proper preparation, the test should be facile.

(Synonym) Too easy, Simplistic, Glib. (Antonym) Profound.

Faithful (adjective) The people who believe in a religion; exact and accurate; loyal.
- He is a faithful believer who attended Catholic mass every morning.

(Synonym) Trustworthy, Dedicated, Devoted.

Fallacy (noun) A wrong belief; a false or mistaken idea.
- It's a fallacy to think that humans use only about 10 percent of their brainpower.

(Synonym) Misconception, Error, Misjudgment.

Fallow (adjective) Not used for growing crops; not planted; not active or productive.
- The farmers allowed several fields to lie fallow so they could regain nutrients.

(Synonym) Unproductive, Unused, Uncultivated. (Antonym) Cultivated.

Falter (verb) To stop being strong or successful; to begin to fail or weaken.
- I was faltering in front of the audience when playing my favorite piano piece for the Christmas concert.

(Synonym) Fade, Fumble, Hesitate.

Famished (adjective) Very hungry; intensely hungry.
- What's for dinner? I'm famished.

(Synonym) Starving, Lacking, Ravenous.

Fascinated (verb) To cause to be very interested; to be irresistibly attractive.
- She is fascinated by her brother's ability to jump so high.
(Synonym) Captivated, Absorbed, Attracted.

Fastidious (adjective) Difficult to please; wanting to always be clean or neat; having high and often capricious standards; having complex nutritional requirements; liking few things.
- My daughter is a fastidious eater.
(Synonym) Demanding, Picky, Particular. (Antonym) Easygoing.

Fatal (adjective) Causing death, ruin, or failure.
- Bob's fall from the tree proved to be fatal despite the efforts of the ambulance crew.
(Synonym) Deadly, Accidental, Lethal.

Fathom (noun) A unit of length equal to six feet (about 1.8 meters), used to measure the depth of water.
- The lake where the boat was cruising was about six fathoms deep.
(Synonym) Measure, Gauge.

Fatigue (noun) The uniform that soldiers wear when they are doing physical work; the state of being very tired; extreme weariness or exhaustion from labor, exertion, or stress.
- After a long day of work, I have extreme fatigue.
(Synonym) Weariness, Grow weary, Lethargy.

Favor (verb) To prefer; give support or approval to; to show that you like or approve of someone more than others.
- That teacher favors the children who have good grades over the children who have poor grades.
(Synonym) Choose, Esteem, Give preferentiality to. (Antonym) Reject.

Feasible (adjective) Possible to do; capable of being used or dealt with successfully.
- The mayor's plan for a new stadium is not economically feasible.
(Synonym) Achievable, Practical, Realistic. (Antonym) Impossible.

Feeble (adjective) Markedly lacking in strength; indicating weakness.
- The feeble old man was weakened by hunger.
(Synonym) Ineffective, Weak, Frail. (Antonym) Robust.

Feign (verb) To pretend to feel or be affected by something; to give a false appearance of.
- Sarah would often feign illness to get out of class.
(Synonym) Fake, Make believe, Put on.

Feint (noun) A quick movement one makes to trick an opponent.
- It was a feint when he passed the ball to his teammate; in reality, he was shooting to the hoop.
(Synonym) Sham, Maneuver, Fool.

Feline (adjective) Of or relating to the cat family; sleekly graceful.
- The leopard is a species of feline.
(Synonym) Graceful, Slinky, Elegant.

Ferocity (noun) A very fierce or violent quality; the quality or state of being ferocious.
- The small kickboxer's ferocity was often underestimated.
(Synonym) Cruelty, Aggressiveness, Fierceness. (Antonym) Gentleness.

Fetish (noun) A strong and unusual need or desire for something; an object that is believed to have magical powers; a rite or cult of fetish worshipers.
- Her bracelet was a fetish that could supposedly lower her blood pressure.
(Synonym) Talisman, Charm, Obsession.

Fiction (noun) Literature that tells stories that are imagined by the writer; stories that are not real.
- The story of her loss of wages was pure fiction.
(Synonym) Falsehood, Untruth, Novel. (Antonym) Fact.

Filament (noun) A thin thread or hair; thin wire in a light bulb that glows when electricity passes through it.
- Thomas Edison's experiments tested filaments of different materials.
(Synonym) String, Thread, Yarn.

Fiscal (adjective) Of or relating to money and especially to the money of a government, business, or organization.
- The town budget for the forthcoming fiscal year is slightly more than the current year's.
(Synonym) Economic, Financial, Monetary.

Flagrant (adjective) Conspicuously offensive; obviously inconsistent with what is right or proper as to appear to be a flouting of law or morality; very bad, too bad to be ignored.
- The prison camp's condition was a flagrant violation of human rights.
(Synonym) Blatant, Glaring, Scandalous. (Antonym) Covert.

Flatter (verb) To praise someone excessively in a way that is not sincere, from motives of self-interest; to use flattery.
- He flattered the old woman with comments about her youthful appearance.
(Synonym) Compliment, Adulate, Cajole. (Antonym) Insult.

Flighty (adjective) Not serious; likely to forget things or change opinions, without reason; easily excited or frightened.
- The flighty businessman often misplaced his briefcase.
(Synonym) Changeable, Inconsistent, Variable. (Antonym) Dependable.

Florid (adjective) Very fancy or too fancy; having a red or reddish color.
- She had a florid face after a summer vacation in the mountains.
(Synonym) Ornate, Ruddy, Sanguine.

Fluent (adjective) Capable of using a language easily and accurately.
▪ She speaks fluent French and Chinese.
(Synonym) Articulate, Voluble, Flowing, Easy. (Antonym) Halting, Tongue-tied.

Foe (noun) An enemy; one who has personal enmity for another.
▪ The politician's speech was applauded by friend and foe alike.
(Synonym) Adversary, Antagonist, Enemy. (Antonym) Friend.

Foible (noun) A minor fault or shortcoming in someone's character or behavior; weakness.
▪ It is human nature that we all have our little foibles.
(Synonym) Bad habit, Imperfection, Idiosyncrasy. (Antonym) Strength.

Foment (verb) To cause the growth or development of something bad or harmful.
▪ The manager was accused of fomenting racial tension in the workplace.
(Synonym) Incite, Encourage, Instigate.

Forecast (verb) To calculate the future; to predict something, such as weather.
▪ Meteorologists are forecasting rain for this weekend.
(Synonym) Anticipate, Estimate, Project.

Foregone (adjective) Something in the future that is certain to happen or be true.
▪ It's a foregone conclusion that she will retire next year.
(Synonym) Predetermined, Predictable, Preordained. (Antonym) Uncertain.

Former (adjective) Used to say what someone or something was in the past.
▪ The former governor spoke at the school's commencement.
The first one of two things or people that have been mentioned previously.
▪ Of apples and oranges, I prefer the former.
(Synonym) Previous, Ex, Anterior.

Formidable (adjective) Very powerful or strong; deserving serious attention and respect; large or impressive in size or amount.
▪ Last year's champion will be a formidable opponent in the chess competition this weekend.
(Synonym) Awesome, Remarkable, Admirable. (Antonym) Insignificant.

Forswear (verb) To promise to give up or to stop doing something; to reject or renounce under oath.
▪ My dad says he will forswear cigarettes and alcohol as his New Year's resolution.
(Synonym) Abjure, Disown, Reject.

Forthright (adjective) Honest and direct; providing answers or information in a very clear and direct way.
▪ The judge was assumed to be a forthright person.
(Synonym) Upfront, Straightforward, Frank.

Fortify (verb) To strengthen a place by building military defenses; to make stronger.

- Years ago, cities were fortified by building thick, tall walls around them.
(Synonym) Reinforce, Defend, Protect.

Fortnight (noun) A period of fourteen days; two weeks.
- I arrived in the Bahamas a fortnight ago.

Fortunate (adjective) Having good luck; enjoying good fortune; lucky.
- They were fortunate enough to win the lottery.
(Synonym) Privileged, Prosperous, Blessed.

Fraction (noun) A number such as one-half or three-quarters that indicates that one number is being divided by another; a part or amount of something; a piece broken off; fragment.
- The new software allows us to complete the job in a fraction of the time.
(Synonym) Portion, Part, Division.

Fragile (adjective) Easily broken or damaged; very delicate; not strong.
- The package containing fragile items needed special handlings.
(Synonym) Flimsy, Frail, Weak.

Fragrance (noun) A sweet or pleasant odor such as perfume.
- I am using a deodorant with a fragrance of citrus blossom and strawberries.
(Synonym) Cologne, Scent, Aroma.
Fragrant (adjective) Having a pleasant and usually sweet smell.
- The bathroom was fragrant with the scent of dried lavender.
(Synonym) Perfumed, Scented, Aromatic.

Frequent (adjective) Happening often; acting or returning regularly or often.
- Elizabeth likes to read; thus, she is a frequent visitor at her school's library.
(Synonym) Repeated, Habitual, Regular. (Antonym) Rare.

Fret (verb) To worry or be concerned; to become agitated.
- You don't have to fret over the test because it will be easy.
(Synonym) Vex, Upset, Bother.

Friendly (adjective) Acting like a friend; kind and helpful; easy to use or understand.
- The school's environment is friendly and welcoming.
(Synonym) Outgoing, Affable, Amiable. (Antonym) Reserved.

Frock (noun) A long outer garment worn by some Christian monks and friars; a woman's or girl's dress.
- Anna wore a used frock to the party.
(Synonym) Dress, Gown.

Frugal (adjective) Careful about spending money; simple and plain.
- Michelle was very frugal when she was in college.
(Synonym) Thrifty, Economical, Stingy. (Antonym) Prodigal.

Fundamental (adjective) The most important part of something; basic; relating to essential structure, function, or facts.
- The Constitution ensures our fundamental rights.
(Synonym) Essential, Vital, Elemental.

Furl (verb) To wrap or roll, such as a sail or a flag around something.
- They furled the sails before entering the channel.
(Synonym) Curl, Wave, Wind up.

Futile (adjective) Having no result or effect; pointless or useless.
- Your exercise program will be futile if you do not stop eating sugar.
(Synonym) Vain, Unsuccessful, Fruitless. (Antonym) Useful.

Gainful (adjective) Producing gain; making money.
- Her gainful profession allows her to make more money than her peers.
(Synonym) Beneficial, Profitable, Lucrative. (Antonym) Unprofitable.

Gainsay (verb) To declare to be untrue or invalid; to deny or disagree with.
- The judge told the defendant that there is no gainsaying the evidence.
(Synonym) Oppose, Contradict, Refute. (Antonym) Agree.

Gallant (adjective) Showing courage; very brave; showing politeness and respect for women.
- The Fort Dix soldiers were commended for their gallant stand in controlling the terrible situation.
(Synonym) Courteous, Chivalrous, Gracious.

Gallop (noun) The way a horse moves when it is running fast and all four of its feet leave the ground at the same time.
- The horse was at full gallop.

Garble (verb) To cause a word, name, or message to be unclear or confusing.
- Sophia garbled some of the words in her first speech as the president of the school.
(Synonym) Distort, Misunderstand, Twist.

Gargantuan (adjective) Very large in size or amount; gigantic.
- When I go to a restaurant, I always ask for a gargantuan portion.
(Synonym) Colossal, Huge, Enormous.

Garrulous (adjective) Tending to talk a lot; overly talkative.
- My uncle became more garrulous after drinking alcohol.
(Synonym) Verbose, Chatty, Loquacious. (Antonym) Taciturn.

Generic (adjective) Of or relating to a whole group or class.
- The hospital prescribes only generic drugs to the patients.
(Synonym) General, Standard, Basic. (Antonym) Specific.

Generous (adjective) Freely giving or sharing; providing more than what is needed; abundant or ample.
- The school raised its endowment through donations from generous alumni.
(Synonym) Substantial, Lavish, Benevolent. (Antonym) Meager, Stingy.

Genre (noun) A category of artistic, musical, or literary composition characterized by a particular style, form, or content.
- I listen to multiple genres of music, from classic rock to hip-hop.
(Synonym) Type, Category, Genus.

Genteel (adjective) Elegant or graceful in manner or appearance; polite; people who have high social status; aristocratic.
- My classmate is a descendant of a well-known genteel family.
(Synonym) Cultivated, Well-mannered, Refined. (Antonym) Vulgar.

Genuine (adjective) Actual, real, or true; free from hypocrisy or pretense; sincere and honest.
- The signature inside my bag is genuine.
(Synonym) Authentic, Frank, Candid. (Antonym) False.

Ghastly (adjective) Very shocking or horrible; resembling a ghost; filled with fear.
- She has an unpleasant and ghastly attitude.
(Synonym) Frightening, Unpleasant, Dreadful. (Antonym) Pleasant.

Gigantic (adjective) Extremely large; exceeding the usual or expected in size, force, or prominence.
- They have opened a gigantic supermarket in the community.
(Synonym) Oversize, Colossal, Enormous.

Glance (verb) To take a quick look at; to catch a glimpse of.
- I quickly glanced at my watch to see if I was late for the appointment.
(Synonym) Partial view, Peep, Browse.

Glib (adjective) Said or done too easily or carelessly; showing little preparation or thought; lacking depth and substance; nonchalant.
- His glib comment made him appear rude.
(Synonym) Superficial, Facile, Casual. (Antonym) Profound.

Gloat (verb) To show in an improper or selfish way that you are happy with your own success or another person's failure.
- If I win the election, I will call my family and gloat.
(Synonym) Triumph, Rejoice, Take pride.

Gloomy (adjective) Somewhat dark; not bright or sunny; causing feelings of sadness; sad or depressed; low in spirits; not hopeful or promising.
- The winter weather is gloomy.
(Synonym) Morose, Melancholy, Blue.

Gluttony (noun) Excess in eating or drinking; greedy or excessive indulgence.
▪ We should be forgiven for the sin of gluttony during the Thanksgiving holiday.
(Synonym) Rapaciousness, Gourmandizing, Voraciousness.

Gnarled (adjective) Having many twists and hard bumps or knots; to be a source of vexation.
▪ The old woman could not find a shoe to fit her because of her gnarled toes.
(Synonym) Twisted, Crooked, Distorted.

Goad (verb) To urge or force someone to do something; action.
▪ She took her employer to court to goad him into paying her a decent salary.
(Synonym) Provoke, Incite, Prod.

Gouge (verb) To cut a deep hole in something.
▪ My husband accidentally gouged a hole in the wall with his screwdriver.
To make someone pay too much money for something.
▪ During the power outage, the store owner gouged customers on the price of ice.
(Synonym) Overcharge, Scratch, Scoop out.

Grace (noun) A way of moving that is smooth and attractive and not stiff or awkward;
a virtue coming from God; a state of sanctification enjoyed through divine grace.
▪ She handled the death of her husband with grace and dignity.
(Synonym) Elegance, Poise, Decency. (Antonym) Unkindness.

Gracious (adjective) Very polite in a way that shows respect; marked by tact and delicacy.
▪ She is a gracious woman who makes everyone comfortable at her house.
Characterized by charm, good taste, generosity of spirit, and comfort.
▪ The website promotes gracious living.
(Synonym) Kind, Diplomatic, Courteous. (Antonym) Rude.

Grandiose (adjective) Seeming to be impressive but not really possible or practical;
absurd exaggeration.
▪ Plans for the Christmas party were criticized as grandiose.
(Synonym) Lavish, Magnificent, Impressive. (Antonym) Modest.

Gratuitous (adjective) Given unearned or without recompense; not involving a return
benefit, compensation, or consideration; costing nothing; not necessary or appropriate.
▪ The video game was criticized for its gratuitous violence.
(Synonym) Complimentary, Free, Unnecessary.

Grave (noun) A hole in the ground for burying a dead body; a burial place.
▪ We went to the cemetery to visit my aunt's grave.

Grave (adjective) Very serious, requiring or causing serious thought or concern.
▪ Violence is a grave matter at the workplace.
(Synonym) Grim, Solemn, Serious.

Greed (noun) A selfish and excessive desire to have more than is needed.
▪ Some companies are funding their greed by not paying the workers a decent salary.
(Synonym) Gluttony, Voracity, Craving. (Antonym) Moderation.

Gregarious (adjective) Enjoying the company of other people; tending to live in groups.
▪ My daughter is a self-confident young adult; she's outgoing and has a gregarious personality.
(Synonym) Outgoing, Sociable, Extroverted. (Antonym) Shy.

Grim (adjective) Unpleasant or shocking to see or think about; causing feelings of sadness.
▪ This accident serves as a grim reminder of the danger of staying out too late.
(Synonym) Somber, Gloomy, Harsh.

Grimace (noun) A facial expression in which one's mouth and face are twisted in a way that shows disgust, disapproval, or pain.
▪ My daughter always made a painful grimace when she was being vaccinated.
(Synonym) Frown, Long face, Sneer.

Grin (verb) To smile widely; to accept something that you do not like because you have no choice.
▪ I grinned when my manager refused to sign my summer's vacation.
(Synonym) Chuckle, Laugh, Smirk. (Antonym) Frown.

Gruff (adjective) Rough, brusque, stern, or very serious in manner; being deep and harsh.
▪ My math teacher has a gruff voice.
(Synonym) Bad-tempered, Grumpy, Impatient. (Antonym) Friendly.

Guile (noun) The use of clever and usually dishonest methods to achieve something.
▪ He used guile to convince his patients that he was a certified doctor.
(Synonym) Deceit, Cunning, Treachery. (Antonym) Honesty.

Guileless (adjective) Very innocent; naïve.
▪ She grew from a guileless girl into a mature, self-confident woman.
(Synonym) Candid, Frank.

Gullible (adjective) Easily fooled or cheated; quick to believe something that is not true.
▪ The businessman absconded with thousands of dollars from the gullible investors.
(Synonym) Naïve, Innocent, easily deceived.

Gurney (noun) A stretcher bed on a frame with wheels that is used for moving people who are sick or injured.
▪ I was wheeled into surgery on a gurney.

QUIZ 6- MATCH EACH WORD IN THE FIRST COLUMN WITH ITS SYNONYM IN THE SECOND COLUMN. CHECK YOUR ANSWERS IN THE BACK OF THE BOOK.

1. fabricate	a. naive
2. facet	b. economical
3. facile	c. overly talkative
4. famished	d. twisted
5. foe	e. falsify
6. fortify	f. aspect
7. frugal	g. sociable
8. gainful	h. strengthen
9. garrulous	i. spin
10. generic	j. easy
11. gnarled	k. hungry
12. gracious	l. enemy
13. gregarious	m. profitable
14. guileless	n. kind
15. gyrate	0. general

Gyrate (verb) To move back and forth with a circular motion; winding or coiled around; convoluted.
▪ The marching band members are gyrating to the beat of the music in the stadium.
(Synonym) Rotate, Whirl, Spin.

Hallow (adjective) Holy or set apart for holy use; highly respected; venerated.
▪ The Vatican is hallowed as holy.
(Synonym) Sanctified, Revered, Sacred.

Hamlet (noun) A small village.
▪ The hamlet included small groups of houses in a tight-knit community.

Harbinger (noun) Something that shows what is coming.
▪ Sometimes, heat is a harbinger of storm.
(Synonym) Messenger, Herald, Indication.

Hardy (adjective) Able to live through difficult conditions such as a cold winter or a drought.
▪ Kiwis, fig trees, and roses are hardy plants and do not require constant care.
Strong; capable of withstanding adverse conditions.
▪ They chose the hardy young soccer players to send to the World Cup.
(Synonym) Resilient, Healthy, Robust. (Antonym) Frail.

Harsh (adjective) Unpleasant and difficult to accept or experience; severe.
- The human right activists had to intervene to stop the harsh punishment given to hostages.
(Synonym) Punitive, Strict, Cruel. (Antonym) Lenient.

Hasten (verb) To move or act quickly; to urge on.
- The headmaster hastened the construction of the library before the opening of the school.
(Synonym) Accelerate, Rush, Race.

Hastily (adverb) Done or made very quickly.
- The students hastily completed their homework assignments.
(Synonym) Rapidly, Fast, Immediately. (Antonym) Slowly.

Haughty (adjective) The insulting attitude of people who think that they are better, or more important than other people.
- She looked at the waiter with an air of haughty disdain.
(Synonym) Proud, Arrogant, Superior. (Antonym) Humble.

Hazy (adjective) Partly hidden, darkened, or clouded by dust, smoke, or mist; hidden by haze; obscured or made dim.
- Yesterday, I could not go to school because the forest fire made the air too hazy to drive.
(Synonym) Vague, Indistinct, Misty.

Headstrong (adjective) Not willing to do what other people want; very stubborn.
- He was a headstrong activist who did not take no for an answer.
(Synonym) Determined, Obstinate, Imprudent.

Heap (noun) A large, disordered pile of things.
- John sat on the heap of newspaper.
(Synonym) Stack, Load, Pile.

Hectic (adjective) Very busy and filled with activity; characterized by activity, excitement, or confusion.
- She maintained a hectic schedule as an accountant and mother.
(Synonym) Chaotic, Frenetic, Frantic. (Antonym) Calm.

Heir (noun) One who receives or is entitled to receive some endowment from a parent or predecessor; one who inherits or is entitled to inherit.
- Christina was the only heir of her mother's estate.
(Synonym) Successor, Beneficiary, Heritor.

Heirloom (noun) A valuable object that is owned by a family for many years and passed from one generation to another.
- This antique necklace is a family heirloom.
(Synonym) Inheritance, Bequest, Family treasure.

Henchman (noun) A trusted follower or supporter who performs unpleasant, wrong, or illegal tasks for a powerful person such as a politician or criminal.
▪ While he was in jail, the criminal was communicating with his henchman in order to escape.
(Synonym) Right-hand man, Member of a gang.

Herald (verb) To be a sign of something that is beginning to happen or will happen soon; to give notice of.
▪ She is being heralded as the breakout film star of the coming year.
(Synonym) Messenger, Announcer, Bearer of news.

Herbivore (noun) An animal that only eats plants.
▪ A buffalo is a large herbivore.

Herd (noun) A group of certain animals that live or are kept together.
▪ A herd of buffalos grazed on the prairie grass.
(Synonym) Crowd, Group, Pack.

Heritage (noun) The traditions, achievements, and beliefs that are part of the history of a group or nation.
▪ China is a nation with one of the world's richest cultural heritages.
Something transmitted by or acquired from a predecessor.
▪ After the death of my father, I received my portion of our family's heritage.
(Synonym) Legacy, Inheritance, Birthright.

Hiatus (noun) An interruption in time or continuity; a period of time when something such as an activity or program is stopped.
▪ The TV show is on hiatus after the lead actor was caught in a scandal.
(Synonym) Pause, Break, Gap.

Hideous (adjective) Offensive to the senses and especially to sight; exceedingly ugly or disgusting.
▪ The story is about a lovely princess living with a hideous beast.
(Synonym) Dreadful, Gruesome, Repulsive.

Hierarchy (noun) The different levels an organization is divided into; a body of persons in authority.
▪ The hierarchy of the Roman Catholic Church is headed by the pope.
(Synonym) Ladder, Chain of command, Pyramid.

Highwayman (noun) A thief, especially in the past, who stopped travelers on roads and robbed them.
▪ The monks on pilgrimage were set upon by highwaymen.

Hilarity (noun) Noisy fun or laughter; boisterous merriment.
▪ The planning of the upcoming school trip was a source of great hilarity in the classroom.
(Synonym) Amusement, Joviality, Cheerfulness. (Antonym) Sadness.

Historic (adjective) Happening or existing in the past; famous or important in history; having great and lasting importance.
▪ The Statue of Liberty in New York is a historic landmark.
(Synonym) Significant, Famous, Remarkable. (Antonym) Modern.

Hoax (noun) An act that is meant to trick or deceive people.
▪ April Fools Day is a day of hoaxes.
(Synonym) Prank, Fraud, Falsification.

Homage (noun) Expression of high regard respect, or honor; tribute.
▪ We pay homage to our fallen heroes.
(Synonym) Respect, Reverence, Praise.

Homogenize (verb) To reduce the particles of something so they are uniformly small and evenly distributed.
▪ We are working on the issue in order to homogenize education throughout the country.
(Synonym) Standardize, Make the same, Normalize. (Antonym) Distinguish.

Hope (verb) To want something to happen or be true and to think that it could happen or be true.
▪ I hope to visit Europe this summer.
(Synonym) Promise, Expect, Anticipate. (Antonym) Despair.

Horizontal (adjective) Positioned from side to side rather than up and down; parallel to the ground.
▪ "Getting horizontal" was the phrase Bob's dad used for the act of lying down on the couch.

Hostile (adjective) Of or relating to an enemy; showing unfriendly feelings.
▪ The new administration has taken steps to eliminate hostile relations between the United States and Cuba.
(Synonym) Antagonistic, Harsh, Aggressive. (Antonym) Friendly.

Humane (adjective) Marked by compassion, sympathy, and consideration for humankind.
▪ Since the new warden's reforms, conditions in the prison are more humane.
(Synonym) Compassionate, Civilized, Humanitarian.

Humid (adjective) Having a lot of moisture in the air.
▪ It is too humid to ride bicycles today.
(Synonym) Moist, Damp, Tropical. (Antonym) Arid, Dry.

Humility (noun) The quality or state of not thinking you are better than other people; humble.
▪ Displaying humility and remorse, the disgraced athlete returned his trophies.
(Synonym) Self-effacement, Modesty, Shyness. (Antonym) Arrogance.

Humongous (adjective) Extremely large; huge.

- The billionaire's mansion is humongous.

(Synonym) Enormous, Gigantic, Colossal. (Antonym) Tiny.

Humor (noun) The ability to be funny or to be amused by things that are funny.
- My father has a great sense of humor and often laughs.

(Synonym) Wit, Hilarity, Absurdity. (Antonym) Seriousness.

Humus (noun) A brown or black complex variable material resulting from partial decomposition of plant or animal matter and forming the organic portion of topsoil.
- When the plants decayed, humus formed in the soil.

Hydrate (noun) A substance that is formed when water combines with another substance.
- Washing soda is a hydrate composed of sodium, carbon, oxygen, and water.

Hyperbole (noun) Language that describes something as better or worse than it really is; exaggeration.
- In describing her adventure vacation, Jennifer is somewhat given to hyperbole.

(Synonym) Exaggeration, Embellishment.

Hypothesis (noun) An idea or theory that is not proven but that leads to further study or discussion.
- The researchers studied the hypothesis that watching a lot of television reduces a person's ability to sleep.

(Synonym) Theory, Supposition, Assumption.

Hysteria (noun) A state in which one's emotions, such as fear and anger, are so strong that one behaves in an extreme or uncontrolled way.
- When their trip to Disney was canceled, the students were all caught up in the ensuing hysteria.

(Synonym) Panic, Emotion, Excitement. (Antonym) Calm.

Hysterical (adjective) Feeling or showing extreme and uncontrolled emotion; marked by hysteria; very funny.
- We enjoyed the comedic play because it was hysterical.

(Synonym) Distraught, Agitated, Overexcited. (Antonym) Composed.

Ideal (adjective) A standard of perfection, beauty, or excellence; someone who deserves to be imitated or admired; exactly right for a particular purpose, situation, or person; perfect.
- The conference provided us with an ideal opportunity to meet new people.

Existing as a mental image or in fancy imagination only, lacking practicality.
- In an ideal world, there would be no war.

Identical (adjective) Being exactly alike or equal; having such close resemblance as to be essentially the same.
- They are identical twins.

(Synonym) Duplicate, Equal, Matching.

Ignoble (adjective) Formal; not deserving respect; not noble or honorable; characterized by baseness.
- The felon had an ignoble past.
(Synonym) Dishonorable, Shameful, Dastardly. (Antonym) Noble.

Illiterate (adjective) Having little or no education; unable to read or write.
- My grandfather was illiterate; he could neither read nor write.
Having or showing a lack of knowledge about a particular subject.
- I am illiterate when it comes to computers.
(Synonym) Ignorant, Unschooled, Untaught.

Illustrate (verb) To give examples in order to make something easier to understand.
- The teacher illustrated her points with a slideshow.
To provide with pictures intended to explain or decorate.
- The story was illustrated by the students.
(Synonym) Exemplify, Demonstrate, Draw.

Image (noun) The idea that people have about someone or something; a picture that is produced by a camera, artist, or mirror; a reproduction or imitation of the form of a person or thing.
- The scandal has negatively affected the athlete's image.
(Synonym) Icon, Figure, Copy.

Imbue (verb) To cause to be deeply affected by a feeling or to have a certain quality.
- His travel experiences imbued him with a strong sense of giving back.
(Synonym) Instill, Saturate, Suffuse.

Immense (adjective) Very great in size or amount; supremely good.
- The ocean is immense.
(Synonym) Huge, Large, Colossal.

Imminent (adjective) Happening very soon; just around the corner.
- These rare birds are in imminent danger of extinction.
(Synonym) Forthcoming, Coming up, Impending. (Antonym) Distant.

Impassive (adjective) Not showing emotion.
- The impassive singers lacked the energy needed for a great performance.
(Synonym) Expressionless, Aloof, Unfeeling.

Impeach (verb) To charge a public official with a crime committed while in office; to cause doubts about the truthfulness of; to challenge the credibility or validity of.
- The president was nearly impeached and removed from office.
(Synonym) Bring to court, Prosecute, Put on trial.

Impeccable (adjective) Free from fault, blame, or error; not capable of sinning or not liable to sin.
▪ She possesses an impeccable wardrobe that demonstrates her good sense of fashion.
(Synonym) Faultless, Perfect, Spotless.

Impede (verb) To slow the movement, progress, or action of someone or something.
▪ The weight of my bag impeded me as I tried to walk faster.
(Synonym) Obstruct, Hinder, Delay.

Imperative (adjective) Very important; not to be avoided; necessary; expressing a command.
▪ It is imperative that the children be vaccinated to prevent infection.
(Synonym) Vital, Crucial, Compulsory. (Antonym) Optional.

Imperious (adjective) Commanding, domineering, expecting obedience.
▪ My imperious classmate expects everyone to stop to listen to him.
(Synonym) Authoritative, Arrogant, Haughty.

Impish (adjective) Having or showing a playful desire to cause trouble; playful and mischievous.
▪ Watch out for that young boy; he has an impish look.
(Synonym) Mischievous, Naughty, Wicked.

Implement (verb) To make active or effective.
▪ The school system implemented a series of reforms for the after-school program.
(Synonym) Put into practice, Realize, Execute.

Imply (verb) To suggest something without saying or showing it plainly; to express indirectly.
▪ Your remark implies that you think I am lying.
(Synonym) Entail, Involve, Hint.

Import (verb) To bring a product into a country to be sold; to bring into a country from another country.
▪ The company imports fine wines from France to the United States.
(Synonym) Bring in, Introduce, Trade in. (Antonym) Export.

Impose (verb) To force someone to accept.
▪ The king imposed his will on his subjects.
(Synonym) Inflict, Compel, Require.

Impotent (adjective) Lacking power, strength, or vigor.
▪ The efforts of the new leader to govern proved impotent, and he was deposed.
(Synonym) Powerless, Weak, Ineffective. (Antonym) Powerful.

Impress (verb) To cause to feel admiration or interest; to produce a vivid impression.
▪ Your résumé impressed us.
(Synonym) Make an impression, Amaze, Astonish.

Impressive (adjective) Deserving attention, admiration, or respect; making or tending to make a marked impression.
▪ Her independent school application essay was impressive.
(Synonym) Remarkable, Notable, Extraordinary.

Impromptu (adjective) Not prepared ahead of time; made or done without preparation.
▪ Impromptu rallies occurred across France to support freedom of expression.
(Synonym) Unrehearsed, Spontaneous, Ad-lib.

Imprudent (adjective) Not wise or sensible; not prudent; lacking discretion, wisdom, or good judgment.
▪ Imprudent behavior can get you into big trouble.
(Synonym) Reckless, Irresponsible, Unwise.

Impulsive (adjective) Done suddenly and without planning; resulting from a sudden impulse.
▪ His impulsive behavior led to his suspension at school.
(Synonym) Imprudent, Spontaneous, Thoughtless.

Inadequate (noun) Not enough or not good enough; insufficient; not capable.
▪ You should study more because your grades are inadequate for college admission.
(Synonym) Lacking, Inefficient, Scarce.

Inalienable (adjective) Impossible to take away or give; incapable of being alienated, surrendered, or transferred.
▪ Certain rights are inalienable.
(Synonym) Unchallengeable, Absolute, Assured.

Inane (adjective) Very silly or stupid; lacking significance, meaning, or point.
▪ She showed up late at the meeting with some inane excuses.
(Synonym) Empty, Ridiculous, Immature.

Inarticulate (adjective) Not able to express ideas clearly and effectively in speech or writing; not articulate.
▪ I could not understand the essence of her speech because she was inarticulate.
(Synonym) Mumbled, Incoherent, Tongue-tied. (Antonym) Eloquent.

Inauspicious (adjective) Not showing or suggesting that future success is likely; not auspicious.
▪ It was an inauspicious time to open a new business.
(Synonym) Unpromising, Ominous, Unfavorable.

Incentive (noun) Something that encourages a person to do something or to work harder.
▪ The credit card company offered potential customers fifty dollars as an incentive to sign up.
(Synonym) Motivation, Encouragement, Reason.

Incessant (adjective) Continuing without stopping; often used to describe something that is unpleasant or annoying.
- The employee's incessant talking distracted me from my work.
(Synonym) Continuous, Constant, Persistent. (Antonym) Sporadic.

Incite (verb) To cause someone to act in an angry, harmful, or violent way.
- The victim had done nothing to incite the attackers.
(Synonym) Provoke, Stimulate, Rouse.

Inclement (adjective) Having rain and storms; stormy; lacking mildness.
- The outdoor concert was postponed due to inclement weather.
(Synonym) Intemperate, Windy, Severe.

Incorrigible (adjective) Not able to be corrected, changed, or reformed.
- He was an incorrigible drunk; he could not give up his habit.
(Synonym) Unruly, Incurable, Hopeless.

Incredible (adjective) Difficult or impossible to believe.
- It is incredible to me that he could be a successful singer with his raspy voice.
Extremely good, great, or large; amazing, extraordinary.
- He has put an incredible amount of work into his college application.
(Synonym) Implausible, Extraordinary, Inconceivable.

Increment (noun) A usually small amount or degree by which something is made larger or greater; something gained or added.
- Students should increase their vocabulary by an increment of two words a day.
(Synonym) Increase, Addition, Augmentation. (Antonym) Decline.

Indecent (adjective) Not appropriate or proper; using language that people find grossly improper or offensive.
- Several of the students at the dance were wearing skimpy outfits that the chaperones deemed indecent.
(Synonym) Offensive, Rude, Improper.

Indefatigable (adjective) Able to work for a very long time without becoming tired; incapable of being fatigued; tireless.
- He is an indefatigable tour guide; I once saw him give four tours in a row.
(Synonym) Untiring, Flagging, Inexorable.

Indicate (verb) To direct attention to by pointing; to show that something exists or is true.
- Studies indicate that students who study in advance get better grades in class.
(Synonym) Designate, Point out, Specify.

Indispensable (adjective) Extremely important and absolutely necessary, essential; not subject to being set aside or neglected.
- Nowadays, a computer is an indispensable tool for students.

(Synonym) Vital, Essential, Necessary.

Industrious (adjective) Working very hard, not lazy; constantly active or occupied; diligent.
▪ Amenise is an industrious worker, producing more than her coworkers.
(Synonym) Hardworking, Productive, Conscientious. (Antonym) Indolent.

Industry (noun) The habit of working hard and steadily; the process of making products by using machinery and factories.
▪ She is a model in her industry given how diligently and effectively she works.
(Synonym) Manufacturing, Production, Diligence.

Inept (adjective) Lacking skill or ability; not done well; lacking in fitness or aptitude; unfit; lacking sense or reason; foolish.
▪ She is an inept lawyer who never wins cases.
(Synonym) Incompetent, Inexpert, Clumsy. (Antonym) Competent.

Inextricable (adjective) Impossible to separate; closely joined or related.
▪ There is an inextricable link between happiness and good health.
Forming a maze or tangle from which it is impossible to escape.
(Synonym) Complicated, Complex, Inseparable. (Antonym) Simple.

Infamous (adjective) Well-known for being bad; known for evil acts or crimes; having a reputation of the worst kind.
▪ The city was infamous for poverty and crime.
(Synonym) Notorious, Recognized, Legendary.

Inflammable (adjective) Capable of being set on fire and of burning quickly; flammable.
▪ Gasoline is highly inflammable.
(Synonym) Incendiary, Combustible, Ignitable.

Inhabit (verb) To live in a place; to have residence in a place; to be present in something.
▪ The native peoples once inhabited the island.
(Synonym) Dwell in, Occupy, Reside in.

Inhibit (verb) To keep someone from doing what he or she wants to do; to suppress or prevent.
▪ The medicine inhibits the growth of cancer cells.
(Synonym) Slow down, Restrain, Reduce.

Initiate (verb) To cause to begin; to introduce to a new interest or activity.
▪ We will initiate the swearing-in ceremony for the new recruits on Sunday.
(Synonym) Open , Commence, Start.

Innocuous (adjective) Not likely to bother or offend anyone.
▪ The doctor's questions were innocuous.
(Synonym) Inoffensive, Harmless, Innocent.

Innovate (verb) To begin something new; to make changes; to have new ideas about how something can be done.
- The development center supports efforts to innovate in the computer industry.
(Synonym) Modernize, Originate, Renovate. (Antonym) Stagnate.

Inopportune (adjective) Not suitable or right for a particular situation, inconvenient; done or happening at the wrong time.
- The rainstorm came at an inopportune moment; no one had an umbrella.
(Synonym) Unfortunate Untimely, Inconvenient.

Inquire (verb) To ask a question; to seek information by questioning; to investigate.
- I am inquiring as to whether the school is hiring any teachers.
(Synonym) Query, Request, Find out.

Inquiry (noun) A request for information; the act of asking questions in order to gather or collect information.
- After the plane crashed, the government launched an inquiry to discover the cause.
(Synonym) Query, Investigation, Examination.

Inquisitive (adjective) Tending to ask questions; having a desire to know or learn more; curious.
- Elizabeth has an inquisitive mind; she is always asking questions.
(Synonym) Interested, Probing, Noisy.

Insane (adjective) Mentally disordered; exhibiting insanity.
- The lawyer argues that his client is insane and as a result cannot stand trial.
(Synonym) Foolish, Senseless, Unreasonable.

Insanity (noun) Severe mental illness; the condition of being insane.
- Master artist Vincent van Gogh experienced periods of insanity.
(Synonym) Irrationality, Folly, Madness.

Inscribe (verb) To write, engrave, or cut words as a lasting record, often in stone or jewelry.
- The jeweler inscribed Vienna's name on her new bracelet.
(Synonym) Carve, Etch, Mark.

Insensitive (adjective) Not sensitive; showing that one does not know or care about the feelings of other people; lacking feeling or tact.
- Politicians must not be insensitive to the needs of their constituents.
(Synonym) Unfeeling, Uncaring, Insensible.

Insinuate (verb) To communicate something bad or insulting in an indirect way.
- I wish he would tell me clearly what he means rather than insinuating something.
(Synonym) Imply, Suggest, Indicate.

Insipid (adjective) Not interesting or exciting; boring; lacking strong flavor; bland; lacking in qualities that stimulate or challenge.
▪ Plain water is insipid, inodorous, and colorless.
(Synonym) Dull, Colorless, Tame.

Insolent (adjective) Having or showing a lack of respect for other people; rude or impolite.
▪ The boy was punished for his insolent behavior.
(Synonym) Impudent, Impertinent, Disrespectful. (Antonym) Respectful.

Insolvent (adjective) Not having enough money to pay debts.
▪ The company has become insolvent and may cease operations.
(Synonym) Bankrupt, Broke, Ruined.

Insomnia (noun) The condition of not being able to sleep; inability to get enough sleep.
▪ She suffers from insomnia and spends most nights awake.
(Synonym) Sleeplessness, Wakefulness, Restlessness.

Inspire (verb) To make someone want to do something; to stimulate to creativity or action.
▪ Her grandmother inspired her to write her first novel.
(Synonym) Motivate, Encourage, Instigate.

Instill (verb) To gradually cause to have an attitude or feeling; to impart gradually.
▪ They instilled a love of music in their children.
(Synonym) Inspire, Encourage, Inculcate.

Intact (adjective) Not broken or damaged; having every part.
▪ Our friendship remained intact, even after more than forty years.
(Synonym) Complete, Unbroken, Undamaged.

Interment (noun) The act of burying a dead person; burial.
▪ The veteran's internment will be at the national cemetery.
(Synonym) Burial, Funeral, Entombment.

Intermittent (adjective) Starting, stopping, and starting again; not constant or steady; at irregular intervals.
▪ The party was canceled due to intermittent rain showers all day.
(Synonym) Sporadic, Erratic, Discontinuous.

Intervene (verb) Occur in time between events; to become involved in something such as a conflict in order to have an influence on what happens.
▪ The military had to intervene to restore order.
(Synonym) Arbitrate, Interfere, Intercede.

Intramural (adjective) Existing or occurring within the limits of a school; contested only within the student body.
▪ Within the school, many students participated in intramural sports.

(Synonym) Internal, In-house.

Intrepid (adjective) Feeling no fear; very bold or brave.
▪ The intrepid explorer traveled all over Europe with only her backpack and guidebook.
(Synonym) Courageous, Fearless, Valiant. (Antonym) Cowardly.

Intrigue (verb) To make secret plans; secret arrangement; plotting.
▪ They were arrested for intriguing against the government.
(Synonym) Conspire, Machinate.

Introvert (noun) A reserved or shy person; a quiet person who does not find it easy to talk to other people.
▪ At the party, the introvert remained in the corner.
(Synonym) Recluse, Loner. (Antonym) Extrovert.

Inundate (verb) To cover with a flood of water, overflow.
▪ Rising sea levels inundated Île Sainte-Marguerite.
(Synonym) Engulf, Flood, Overwhelm.

Invaluable (adjective) Extremely valuable or useful; valuable beyond estimation; priceless.
▪ Sebastien went to China this spring; the trip was an invaluable experience.
(Synonym) Priceless, Precious, Vital.

Invention (noun) The action of making something new, typically a process or device.
▪ Thomas Edison's most famous invention is the light bulb.
(Synonym) Innovation, Originality, Creation.

Invigorate (verb) To give life and energy to someone or something; to animate.
▪ Every morning, I drink a cup of coffee to invigorate myself.
(Synonym) Revitalize, Energize, Refresh.

Irate (adjective) Arising from anger; very angry.
▪ My parents became irate when I did not clean my room after their third request.
(Synonym) Annoyed, Irritated, Furious. (Antonym) Calm.

Ire (noun) Intense and usually openly displayed anger.
▪ The police officer directed his ire at the passerby who witnessed the incident.
(Synonym) Annoyance, Rage, Fury. (Antonym) Calmness.

Irregular (adjective) Not normal or usual; not following the usual rules about what should be done; lacking continuity or regularity, especially of occurrence or activity.
▪ He has a very irregular work schedule; it is impossible to know when he will get around to something.
(Synonym) Uneven, Intermittent, Sporadic.

Irrelevant (adjective) Not important or relating to what is being discussed; not relevant; inapplicable.
▪ Your comments were irrelevant to our debate.
(Synonym) Inappropriate, Unrelated, Not pertinent.

Irritable (adjective) Becoming angry or annoyed easily; capable of being irritated; easily exasperated or excited.
▪ After a long day at school and fencing practice, I came home feeling exhausted and irritable.
(Synonym) Bad-tempered, Grouchy, Petulant.

Itinerant (adjective) Traveling from place to place; staying in a place for only a short amount of time.
▪ He spent his life as an itinerant preacher; he could not settle on a single congregation.
(Synonym) Migrant, Wandering, Nomadic. (Antonym) Settled.

QUIZ 7- MATCH EACH WORD IN THE FIRST COLUMN WITH ITS SYNONYM IN THE SECOND COLUMN. CHECK YOUR ANSWERS IN THE BACK OF THE BOOK.

1. harbinger	a. stubborn
2. haughty	b. traveling
3. headstrong	c. messenger
4. herald	d. essential
5. homage	e. diligence
6. hostile	f. creation
7. hyperbole	g. start
8. identical	h. respect
9. incite	i. exaggeration
10. indispensable	j. arrogant
11. industry	k. announcer
12. initiate	l. sporadic
13. invention	m. unfriendly
14. irregular	n. duplicate
15. itinerant	o. provoke

Jeopardy (noun) Exposure to loss or danger; peril (usually, "in jeopardy")
▪ Eating too much sugar could place your health in serious jeopardy.
(Synonym) Danger, Risk, Difficulty.

Joggle (verb) To shake slightly; to move shakily or jerkily.
▪ She joggled the toddler up and down.
(Synonym) Jiggle, Shake, Knock.

Jollity (noun) A happy and cheerful quality or state; the quality or state of being jolly; a festive gathering.
- Christmas is a season of jollity.
(Synonym) Fun, Hilarity, Merriment. (Antonym) Seriousness.

Jovial (adjective) Good-humored; full of happiness and joy; cheerful.
- He is a jovial man.
(Synonym) Merry, Jolly, Happy. (Antonym) Miserable.

Jubilant (adjective) Feeling or expressing great joy; very happy; exultant.
- The family had a jubilant celebration when my brother graduated from college.
(Synonym) Triumphant, Thrilled, Euphoric.

Jubilee (noun) A special anniversary, such as a twenty-fifth or fiftieth anniversary; a season of celebration.
- Last year, my parents celebrated their silver jubilee.
(Synonym) Commemoration, Celebration, Festival.

Jumbo (adjective) Very large; a very large specimen of its kind; larger than average.
- The fries from the fast-food restaurant are sold in small, medium, large, and jumbo sizes.
(Synonym) Gigantic, Huge, Mammoth. (Antonym) Tiny.

Juxtapose (verb) To place different things together in order to create an interesting effect or to show how they are the same or different.
- Heather's writing juxtaposed love and hate.
(Synonym) Contrast, Compare, Place side by side. (Antonym) Distance.

Keen (adjective) Quick to understand.
- Dogs are keen animals, because they start to learn commands in the first couple of months.
(Synonym) Clever, Sharp, Intelligent.

Keeper (noun) A person who watches, guards, or takes care of something.
- He works as a keeper of a golf course.
(Synonym) Warden, Curator, Caretaker.

Keg (noun) A small barrel or cask; a barrel for holding or serving something such as beer.
- We used up an entire keg of beer at the party.
(Synonym) Barrel, Cask, Drum.

Kiln (noun) An oven or furnace used for processing by hardening or burning a substance such as pottery.
- His new electric kiln left the potter with a cord of unused firewood.

Kinesiology (noun) The study of the principles of mechanics and anatomy in relation to human movement.
- He focused his studies of human movement through kinesiology.

Knack (noun) An ability, talent, or special skill needed to do something; clever.
- He is articulate and has a knack for public speaking.
(Synonym) Aptitude, Capacity, Propensity.

Lachrymose (adjective) Tending to cause tears; mournful.
- The lachrymose leading actor had the theatergoers awash in tears.
(Synonym) Tearful, Crying, Weepy. (Antonym) Cheerful.

Lackadaisical (adjective) Feeling or showing a lack of interest or enthusiasm; lacking life, spirit, or zest; languid.
- The coach did not approve of the team's lackadaisical approach to the game.
(Synonym) Careless, Lazy, Relaxed. (Antonym) Energetic.

Lament (verb) To express sorrow and regret; mourn aloud; wail.
- He lamented the loss of his business partner.
(Synonym) Grieve, Moan, Weep. (Antonym) Celebrate.

Lampoon (noun) A piece of writing or a cartoon that mocks or makes fun of a well-known person or thing.
- The cartoon was a lampoon of the disgraced congressman.
(Synonym) Sketch, Satire, Caricature.

Latitude (noun) Distance north or south of the equator measured in degrees, up to ninety degrees.
- The lines of latitude run horizontally on the globe.
Freedom to choose how to act or what to do.
- Students are allowed considerable latitude in choosing the topic for the term paper.
(Synonym) Leeway, Autonomy, Opportunity.

Laud (verb) To praise highly, especially in public.
- The headmaster lauded the students who made a commitment to community service.
(Synonym) Applaud, Acclaim, Mention. (Antonym) Denigrate.

Lavish (adjective) Giving or using a large amount of something; abundance; prodigal.
- He is a lavish donor to the school.
(Synonym) Extravagant, Plentiful, Copious. (Antonym) Frugal.

Lax (adjective) Not careful enough; not strict enough; deficient in firmness; slack.
- The prisoners escaped due to lax security in the prison laundry.
(Synonym) Negligent, Laid back, Lenient. (Antonym) Strict.

Lecture (noun) A talk, discourse, or speech given before an audience or class, especially for instruction about a particular subject.
- The school invited the former secretary of state to deliver a lecture on foreign service.
A talk that criticizes someone's behavior in an angry or serious way.
- I gave her a lecture on honesty.

(Synonym) Address, Sermon, Reprimand.

Leery (adjective) Feeling or showing a lack of trust in someone or something.
▪ They were leery of their neighbors' involvement in gang violence.
(Synonym) Wary, Suspicious, Skeptical. (Antonym) Confident.

Legitimate (adjective) Allowed by rules or law; conforming to recognized principles or accepted rules and standards.
▪ Legitimate means for acquiring wealth are sometimes not the case.
Born to a father and mother who are married; lawfully begotten; born in wedlock; having full filial rights and obligations by birth.
▪ The king had no legitimate children.
(Synonym) Genuine, Authentic, Legal. (Antonym) Spurious.

Lenient (adjective) Tolerant in terms of punishment from a person of authority.
▪ My homeroom teacher is lenient.
(Synonym) Soft, Relaxed, Easygoing.

Lethargy (noun) A lack of energy or a lack of interest in doing things; a lethargic feeling or state.
▪ She snapped out of her lethargy and began studying for final exams.
(Synonym) Exhaustion, Inactivity, Fatigue. (Antonym) Energy.

Lexicon (noun) A dictionary; the words used in a language by an individual or group of people.
▪ "Selfie" is a new term that has entered the general lexicon.
(Synonym) Vocabulary, Wordlist, Glossary.

Liaison (noun) A person who helps organizations or groups work together and provide information to each other; a close bond or connection; interrelationship; the pronunciation of an otherwise absent consonant sound at the end of the first of two consecutive words, the second of which begins with a vowel sound and follows without pause.
▪ He worked as a liaison between the Departments of Finance and Accounting.
(Synonym) Link, Relationship, Association.

Liberate (verb) To free from control by another person or group; to free a country from domination by a foreign power.
▪ Slaves fought in the Civil War to liberate themselves from slavery.
(Synonym) Release, Unshackle, Set free.

Limber (adjective) Bending easily; capable of being shaped; flexible.
▪ Ballet dancers possess a limber body.
(Synonym) Supple, Nimble, Loose. (Antonym) Stiff.

Limpid (adjective) Perfectly clear, transparent, serene, and untroubled; pellucid; simple in style.

- The limpid lake reflected the vivid autumn foliage like a mirror.
(Synonym) Translucent, Pellucid, Crystal. (Antonym) Opaque.

Linger (verb) To stay somewhere beyond the usual or expected time.
- He lingered with his friends at the airport and missed his flight to Hong Kong.
(Synonym) Loiter, Dawdle, Hang around.

Litigant (noun) A person who is involved in a lawsuit.
- None of the litigants were present for the verdict.
(Synonym) Plaintiff, Complainant, Accuser.

Lofty (adjective) Rising to a great height; very tall and impressive.
- A lofty mountain loomed in the background.
Elevated in character and spirit; noble.
- He set lofty goals for his career such as becoming CEO.
Showing the insulting attitude of people who think that they are better, smarter, or more important than others.
- The newly elected official spoke with a lofty air.
(Synonym) Superior, Distinguished, Arrogant. (Antonym) Humble.

Logo (noun) A symbol that is used to identify a company and that appears on its product.
- The famous Olympic logo makes it easy for customers to recognize the brand.
(Synonym) Emblem, Symbol, Design.

Lucid (adjective) Very clear and easy to understand; having full use of one's faculties; sane.
- My grandmother has remained lucid throughout her illness.
(Synonym) Articulate, Well-spoken, Coherent. (Antonym) Incoherent.

Lucrative (adjective) Producing money or wealth; profitable.
- The restaurant proved to be so lucrative that the owner opened a second one.
(Synonym) Well-paid, Rewarding, Beneficial. (Antonym) Unprofitable.

Ludicrous (adjective) Very foolish; ridiculous; amusing or laughable through obvious absurdity or exaggeration.
- It is ludicrous to think that the answer to terrorist attacks is for everyone to carry a weapon.
(Synonym) Absurd, Farcical, Stupid. (Antonym) Sensible.

Lugubrious (adjective) Full of sadness or sorrow; very sad especially in an exaggerated or insincere way.
- The funeral was lugubrious and left me in terrible sadness.
(Synonym) Depressing, Melancholy, Miserable. (Antonym) Cheerful.

Lunar (adjective) Of, relating to, or resembling the moon; measured by the moon's revolution.
- A lunar eclipse occurs when the Earth's shadow falls upon the moon.
(Synonym) Crescent, Lunate, Astral.

Lunatic (adjective) An insane person; one who behaves in a very foolish way.
- She was driving like a lunatic before being pulled over by the police.
(Synonym) Outrageous, Crazy, Mad. (Antonym) Sensible.

Lunge (verb) To make a forward movement using a part of the body or a weapon.
- The fencer lunged at his opponent but missed his mark.
(Synonym) Attack, Thrust, Swing.

Lyrical (adjective) Having an artistically beautiful or expressive quality.
- Her lyrical dance piece moved the audience.
(Synonym) Emotional, Inspired, Musical.

Magnitude (noun) The importance, quality, size, extent, or caliber of something.
- The discovery of penicillin was an event of great magnitude.
A number that shows the brightness of a star or the power of an earthquake.
- An earthquake of 8.7 magnitude devastated the region.
(Synonym) Greatness, Degree, Importance. (Antonym) Triviality.

Mail (noun) Letters or packages sent from one person to another; a kind of armor made of many small pieces of metal that are linked together; a hard enclosing covering of an animal such as a tortoise.
- The knight wore a coat of chain mail.
(Synonym) Delivery, Transmit, Armor.

Maladroit (adjective) Lack of dexterity; very awkward; not skillful; lacking adroitness; inept.
- The mayor has been harshly criticized for his maladroit handling of the scandal.
(Synonym) Gauche, Clumsy, Graceless. (Antonym) Dexterous, Adroit.

Malady (noun) A disease or illness; an unwholesome or disordered condition; sickness.
- She died after suffering from a terrible malady.
(Synonym)Disorder, Condition, Malaise.

Malcontent (noun) A person who is always unhappy or angry about something; discontented person; one who is in active opposition to an established order or government; rebel.
- My coworker was such a malcontent that she got fired after complaining so much at work.
(Synonym) Discontent, Disgruntled, Dissatisfied. (Antonym) Happy.

Malice (noun) A desire to cause harm, pain, injury, or distress to another person.
- He was charged with malice, murder, and cruelty to children.
In law, used to describe a criminal act that was deliberately planned to cause harm to someone without legal justification or excuse.
- She acted with malice aforethought.
(Synonym) Spite, Hatred, Malevolence. (Antonym) Kindness.

Malicious (adjective) Having or showing a desire to cause harm to another person.
- Carla engaged in malicious behavior; she was always angry and seeking revenge.

(Synonym) Hateful, Spiteful, Malevolent. (Antonym) Kind.

Malignant (adjective) Very serious and dangerous, designating an abnormal growth that tends to spread in a rapid and uncontrolled way that can cause death.
▪ She received the news from her doctor that her tumor is a highly malignant form of cancer.
(Synonym) Deadly, Cancerous, Spreading. (Antonym) Benign.

Malleable (adjective) Capable of being extended, stretched, or bent into different shapes by beating with a hammer or by the pressure of rollers.
▪ Copper is a malleable metal.
Capable of being easily changed or influenced; having a capacity for adaptive change.
▪ It is easier to learn when the mind is young and malleable.
(Synonym) Changeable, Supple, Flexible. (Antonym) Rigid.

Mammoth (noun) Something giant, very large, immense of its kind; huge; a very large, hairy elephant that lived in ancient times with long tusks that curved upward.
▪ The small business she started has now become a mammoth in the industry.
(Synonym) Enormous, Immense, Colossal. (Antonym) Tiny.

Mandatory (adjective) Required by law or rule; obligatory; containing or constituting a command.
▪ The school made it mandatory that all students play a sport.
(Synonym) Obligatory, Required, Compulsory. (Antonym) Optional.

Maneuver (noun) A clever or skillful action or movement; military activities that are done for training.
▪ In a skillful maneuver, his enemies tricked him into betraying his friends.
(Synonym) Exercise, Trick, Contrivance.

Mangle (verb) To injure or damage with deep disfiguring wounds by cutting, tearing, or crushing.
▪ Her face was mangled by the monkey.
To ruin because of a lack of skill; make incoherent especially through ineptitude or ignorance.
▪ The newspaper mangled the story with lies and propaganda.
(Synonym) Crush, Mutilate, Contort.

Mannerism (noun) A person's particular way of talking or moving.
▪ We were happy to find our biological parents, who have the same mannerisms as we do.
(Synonym) Gesture, Trait, Characteristic.

Mannerly (adjective) Behaving politely while with other people; showing good manners.
▪ A mannerly young woman deferred to her elders.
(Synonym) Well-behaved, Respectable, Well-mannered.

Manuscript (noun) The original copy of a play, book, or piece of music before being published; written by hand.

- After his death, the author's family found the manuscript of his last book.
(Synonym) Document, Text, Script.

Marquee (noun) A covered structure over the entrance to a building such as a hotel or theater; a sign over the entrance to a theater that shows the name of the show, movie, or play, and the names of the main performers.
- She will look at the theater's marquee to see what movie is playing tonight.
(Synonym) Pavilion, Canvas, Canopy.

Marvel (noun) Extremely good; skillful; a wonderful or marvelous person or thing; one that causes wonder or astonishment; intense surprise or interest.
- The citadel Acropolis in Athens is a marvel of engineering.
(Synonym) Phenomenon, Miracle, Spectacle.

Masquerade (noun) A party at which people wear masks and often costumes; a way of appearing or behaving that is not true or real.
- The election was all just a masquerade.
(Synonym) Pretense, Cover-up, Concealment.

Massive (adjective) Very large and heavy; solid.
- Elephants are massive animals.
(Synonym) Giant, Huge, Enormous.

Maudlin (adjective) Showing or expressing too much emotion, especially in a foolish or annoying way; effusively or tearfully sentimental.
- After her friend moved to China, she became maudlin, crying for any reason.
(Synonym) Overemotional, Weepy, Oversentimental. (Antonym) Unemotional.

Mayhem (noun) Actions that hurt people and destroy things; a scene or situation that involves a lot of violence or disorder.
- There was mayhem on the street after the protest.
(Synonym) Chaos, Turmoil, Anarchy. (Antonym) Order.

Maze (noun) A complicated and confusing system of connected passages.
- The federal buildings are a maze of regulations and security checks for visitors.
(Synonym) Labyrinth, Web, Bewilder.

Meager (adjective) Lacking in quality or quantity.
- The meager dinner left me looking for more food upon returning home.
(Synonym) Insufficient, Paltry, Derisory. (Antonym) Plentiful.

Meander (verb) To have a lot of curves instead of going in a straight or direct line; to follow a winding course; to wander about without fixed direction.
- We meandered around the city, taking the time to go window-shopping without a clear destination.
To go from one topic to another without any clear direction.

▪ The history teacher meandered from topic to topic during the lecture.
(Synonym) Roam, Deviate, Twist. (Antonym) Rush.

Meddlesome (adjective) Interfering with the activities and concerns of other people in an unwanted or unwelcome way; inclined to meddle.
▪ My neighbor is a meddlesome woman; she always gets involved in other people's business.
(Synonym) Intrusive, Nosy, Officious. (Antonym) Detached.

Meek (adjective) Having a quiet and gentle nature; easily told what to do; not wanting to argue with other people.
▪ As a result of his meek personality, Michael took the blame for something he was not even involved in.
(Synonym) Docile, Weak, Submissive.

Melancholic (adjective) Very sad; gloomy; tending to depress the spirits; saddening.
▪ She is listening to melancholic music.
(Synonym) Miserable, Morose, Nostalgic. (Antonym) Cheerful.

Melodious (adjective) Having a pleasing melody; having or making a pleasant musical sound.
▪ She sang in tune and with a melodious voice.
(Synonym) Harmonious, Tuneful, Pleasant. (Antonym) Harsh.

Melody (noun) A pleasing series of musical notes that form the main part of a song or piece of music.
▪ She claims that the melody comes before the words when writing her songs.
(Synonym) Tune, Strain, Descant.

Mendicant (noun) Someone who lives by asking others for money or food.
▪ Wandering mendicants were members of a religious order that combined monastic life and outside religious activity and who originally owned neither personal nor community property.
(Synonym) Indigent, Beggar, Panhandler.

Mentor (noun) A trusted counselor or guide; tutor; coach.
▪ The school's basketball coach is my close friend and mentor.
(Synonym) Supporter, Teacher, Advisor.

Merit (noun) Character or conduct deserving reward, honor, or esteem; a good quality or feature that deserves to be praised; achievement.
▪ The scholarship will be given based on merit.
(Synonym) Value, Excellence, Distinction.

Mesmerize (verb) To hold the attention of someone entirely; to interest or amaze someone so much that nothing else is seen or noticed; hypnotize.
▪ I was mesmerized by the talent of the circus performers.
(Synonym) Captivate, Enthrall, Excite. (Antonym) Bore.

Metamorphosis (noun) A major change; change in some animals or insects that happens as they become an adult.
▪ Dragonflies undergo metamorphosis in three stages during their life cycle.
(Synonym) Transformation, Conversion, Mutation.

Meticulous (adjective) Very careful about doing something in an extremely accurate and exact way.
▪ My accountant is meticulous, paying extreme attention to details.
Marked by extreme or excessive care in the consideration or treatment of details.
▪ My science teacher is a meticulous researcher; she takes care to consider every possibility.
(Synonym) Finicky, Scrupulous, Detailed. (Antonym) Careless.

Migrate (verb) To move from one country or place to another.
▪ He migrated from the United States to Japan.
(Synonym) Journey, Voyage, Travel.

Mince (verb) To cut or chop into very small pieces.
▪ I recently bought a kitchen gadget to mince onions, peppers, and garlic.
To walk with quick, short steps in a way that does not seem natural and that is often meant to be funny; to speak in a very direct and honest way without worrying that you may be offending someone.
▪ The candidate minced no words in the electoral debate.
(Synonym) Shred, Crumble, Hash.

Minutiae (noun) Small or minor details.
▪ The parents record all the minutiae of their son's daily life.
(Synonym) Finer points, Intricacies, Trivia.

Mirror (noun) A piece of glass that reflects images; something that gives a true representation; an exemplary model/reflection; illustration.
▪ Captain John Smith's literary work is a mirror of American culture.
(Synonym) Glass, Image.

Misanthrope (noun) A person who does not like other people; a person who hates or distrusts humankind.
▪ Eva lived alone and was a known misanthrope who did not like to help others and refused to give to charity.
(Synonym) Pessimist, Recluse, Loner. (Antonym) Philanthropist.

Mischief (noun) Behavior or activity that is annoying but not meant to cause serious harm or damage.
▪ The president's son was charged for disorderly conduct and criminal mischief.
A playful desire to cause trouble; action that annoys or irritates.
(Synonym) Malice, Naughtiness, Misbehavior.

Misconstrue (verb) To understand something incorrectly; to interpret erroneously.

- My intentions of doing a good deed were misconstrued.
(Synonym) Misinterpreted, Misunderstood, Misread.

Misdemeanor (noun) A crime that is not serious.
- The young man was charged with jaywalking, a misdemeanor.
(Synonym) Crime, Offense, Violation.

Miser (noun) A person who hates to spend money; a very stingy person.
- The mean-spirited old miser refused to buy his children new shoes.
(Synonym) Cheapskate, Scrooge, Hoarder.

Mitigate (verb) To cause to become less harsh or hostile; less severe, harmful, or painful; mollify.
- Donations were given to help mitigate the effects of the catastrophe.
(Synonym) Alleviate, Lessen, Ease. (Antonym) Aggravate.

Mnemonic (adjective) Intended to assist memory; of or relating to memory; something such as a word, sentence, or song that helps people remember something, such as a rule or a list of names)
- PEMDAS is used as a mnemonic device for remembering the order of operations in a mathematical expression: Parentheses, Exponents, Multiplication, Division, Addition, and Subtraction.
(Synonym) Reminder, Prompt, Memory aid.

Monotonous (adjective) Used to describe something that is boring because it is always the same; uttered or sounded in one unvarying tone; marked by a sameness of pitch and intensity.
- She sang in a monotonous voice.
(Synonym) Dull, Repetitious, Tedious. (Antonym) Varied.

Moral (adjective) Concerning to what is right and wrong in human behavior; agreeing with a standard of right behavior.
- The student prided himself on being a moral person.
(Synonym) Ethical, Principled, Upright.

Morbid (adjective) Relating to unpleasant subjects such as death; not healthy or normal.
- He has a morbid taste in art.
(Synonym) Macabre, Morose, Gloomy. (Antonym) Cheerful.

Mortify (verb) To cause someone to feel very embarrassed or foolish.
- As a teenager, I was mortified when my parents showed up at my senior prom.
(Synonym) Degrade, Humiliate, Put down.

Mourn (verb) To feel great sadness because someone has died; to express grief or sorrow for.
- Thousands of people mourned the star's death.
(Synonym) Grieve, Lament, Bemoan. (Antonym) Rejoice.

Mousy (adjective) Shy and quiet; of, relating to, or resembling a mouse; dull brown in color.
- The mousy little girl grew up to become a self-confident singer.
(Synonym) Bashful, Stealthy, Timid.

Mundane (adjective) Relating to ordinary life on Earth rather than to spiritual things; commonplace.
- Despite her mundane demeanor, she always goes to church to pray.
(Synonym) Ordinary, Boring, Banal. (Antonym) Exotic.

Munificent (adjective) Very generous; very liberal in giving or bestowing, especially money; lavish.
- Our boss surprised us all with munificent Christmas bonuses.
(Synonym) Bountiful, Openhanded, Charitable. (Antonym) Miserly.

Murky (adjective) Dark, especially due to thick mist or dirt.
- Due to pollution, the water is murky.
(Synonym) Foggy, Gloomy, Muddy. (Antonym) Clear.

Myth (noun) An idea or story that is believed by many people, but that is not true; fairy tale.
- Bloody Mary is a popular American urban myth.
(Synonym) Fiction, Illusion, Legend. (Antonym) Fact.

Mythical (adjective) Existing only in the imagination or myth, imaginary, fictitious.
- Hercules was a mythical hero who was half man and half god.
(Synonym) Legendary, Mythological, Fabled. (Antonym) Factual.

Nadir (noun) The lowest point; the point of the celestial sphere that is directly opposite the zenith.
- After the scandal, the company's credibility reached its nadir.
(Synonym) Base, All time low, Depths. (Antonym) Zenith.

Narrate (verb) To tell a story in detail; to provide spoken commentary for a movie or television show.
- The man narrated his adventure in great detail.
(Synonym) Recount, Relate, Describe.

Negotiate (verb) To discuss something formally in order to make an agreement.
- The union negotiated a fair raise for the city employees.
To get over, through, or around successfully.
- The climber negotiated the treacherous peak.
(Synonym) Exchange, Discuss, Bargain.

Neophyte (noun) A person who has just started learning or doing something, beginner.
- I am a neophyte on computers.

A person who has recently joined a religious group, a new convert.
(Synonym) Novice, Learner, Trainee.

Neutral (adjective) Not supporting either side of an argument, fight, war, or contest; not supporting one political view over another; not expressing strong opinions or feelings.
▪ The tiny country remained neutral throughout the war that ravaged its neighbors.
(Synonym) Not taking sides, Unbiased, Impartial. (Antonym) Biased.

Nib (noun) The pointed metal tip of a pen.
(Synonym) Tip, End, Point.

Nocturnal (adjective) Happening at night; active mainly during the night.
▪ Owls, bats, and fireflies are nocturnal animals.
(Synonym) Nighttime, Night, Nightly. (Antonym) Diurnal.

Noisome (adjective) Very unpleasant or disgusting; noxious; harmful; offensive to the senses and especially to the sense of smell; highly obnoxious or objectionable.
▪ My mother sprayed some air freshener to relieve the noisome smell of garbage in the kitchen.
(Synonym) Malodorous, Disgusting, Repugnant. (Antonym) Pleasant.

QUIZ 8.- MATCH EACH WORD IN THE FIRST COLUMN WITH ITS SYNONYM IN THE SECOND COLUMN. CHECK YOUR ANSWERS IN THE BACK OF THE BOOK.

1. jeopardy	a. musical
2. jubilee	b. change
3. juxtapose	c. peril
4. knack	d. anniversary
5. laud	e. trivia
6. lexicon	f. spiteful
7. lethargy	g. place side by side
8. lyrical	h. dictionary
9. maladroit	i. ability
10. malicious	j. deadly
11. malignant	k. inactivity
12. metamorphosis	l. ordinary
13. mince	m. praise
14. minutiae	n. chop
15. mundane	o. clumsy

Nomad (noun) A member or a group of people who have no fixed residence but move from place to place, usually seasonally and within a well-defined territory.
▪ She lives like a nomad by traveling during the year to Africa, Europe, and the Caribbean.
(Synonym) Wanderer, Itinerant, Migrant.

Nonpartisan (adjective) Not supporting one political party or group over another; free from party affiliation, bias, or designation.
▪ She started a nonprofit, nonpartisan organization aimed at preserving the city's landmarks.
(Synonym) Nonaligned, Independent, Neutral.

Nonchalant (adjective) Relaxed and calm in a way that shows a lack of care or worry.
▪ The police were criticized for being nonchalant in the search for the missing child.
(Synonym) Indifferent, Calm, Insouciant. (Antonym) Concerned.

Nosegay (noun) A small bouquet of flowers; posy.
(Synonym) Bouquet, Bunch, Sprig.

Nostalgia (noun) Pleasure and sadness caused by remembering something from the past and wishing you could experience it again; the state of being homesick.
▪ I was filled with nostalgia when I traveled to Italy to study, until I realized that the place was where I belong.
(Synonym) Melancholy, longing, reminiscence.

Notorious (adjective) Well-known or famous, especially for something bad.
▪ The most notorious criminal in the neighborhood has been captured by the police.
(Synonym) Infamous, Dishonorable, Tarnished. (Antonym) Famous.

Novice (noun) A person who has no previous experience with something; a new member of a religious group who is preparing to take the vows to become a nun or a monk.
▪ She is a novice at playing the violin.
(Synonym) Beginner, Trainee, Neophyte.

Noxious (adjective) Physically harmful or destructive to living things; toxic.
▪ The noxious effects of carbon monoxide can silently kill people while they sleep.
Synonym) Pernicious, Deadly, Lethal. (Antonym) Pleasant.

Nugget (noun) A solid lump of a valuable metal such as gold; a piece of valuable information.
▪ The miner sold several sacks of gold nuggets.
A small, usually round piece of food.
▪ My favorite lunch is chicken nuggets and fries.
(Synonym) Piece, Chunk, Lump.

Numerous (adjective) Existing in large numbers; consisting of great numbers of units or individuals.
▪ Numerous fans are coming to watch the final football game.

(Synonym) Many, Frequent, Abundant. (Antonym) Few.

Oasis (noun) An area in a desert where there is water and plants; something that provides refuge, or pleasant contrast.
▪ Wahoo Bay Beach provided me a much-needed oasis from this hot summer.
(Synonym) Retreat, Sanctuary, Escape.

Oath (noun) Formal and serious promise to tell the truth; under oath; swearword.
▪ In a US court of law, a witness must swear under oath "to tell the truth, the whole truth, and nothing but the truth."
(Synonym) Promise, Pledge, Vow.

Obdurate (adjective) Refusing to do what other people want; not willing to change your opinion; stubborn.
▪ The obdurate donkey refused to move even when prodded.
(Synonym) Obstinate, Inflexible, Adamant. (Antonym) Compliant.

Obedience (adjective) Willing to do what someone tells you to do or to follow a law or rule; willing to obey.
▪ Employees are expected to be obedient to the rules of the workplace.
(Synonym) Compliant, Amenable, Docile. (Antonym) Disobedience.

Obituary (noun) An article in a newspaper about the life of someone who has died recently; a short biographical account.
▪ Soon after her death, they wrote her obituary for the newspaper.
(Synonym) Announcement, Tribute, Eulogy.

Objective (noun) Something you are trying to do or achieve; a goal or purpose.
▪ The objective of the spring break trip was to have the children immersed in a new cultural setting.
(Synonym) Purpose, Intention, Reason.

Obliterate (verb) To destroy completely so that nothing is left.
▪ After the Haitian earthquake in 2010, many homes were obliterated.
(Synonym) Eradicate, Eliminate, Annihilate.

Obscure (adjective) Not well known to most people; not prominent or famous.
▪ He considered the painting for sale by the obscure artist to be a bargain.

Obscure (verb) To make something difficult to understand or know; to hide or cover; conceal.
(Synonym) Dark, Vague, Confuse. (Antonym) Obvious.

Obsolete (adjective) No longer used by anyone because something newer exists.
▪ The invention of the personal computer made the typewriter become obsolete.
(Synonym) Archaic, Old-fashioned, Out-of-date. (Antonym) Up-to-date.

Obstacle (noun) Something that impedes progress or achievement.
▪ Her bad behavior is an obstacle to her success.
(Synonym) Problem, Difficulty, Impediment.

Obstinate (adjective) Refusing to change your behavior or your ideas; difficult to deal with; stubborn.
▪ The manager fired the employees because of their obstinate refusal to implement changes.
(Synonym) Determined, Fixed, Persistent. (Antonym) Compliant.

Obvious (adjective) Easy for the mind to see or notice; easily discovered, seen, or understood.
▪ With her experience, Michelle was the obvious choice for the position.
(Synonym) Clear, Apparent, Evident. (Antonym) Obscure.

Odious (adjective) Causing strong dislike; arousing or deserving hatred or repugnance.
▪ It was one of the most odious crime scenes I have ever seen.
(Synonym) Horrible, Unpleasant, Abominable. (Antonym) Delightful.

Offend (verb) To feel hurt, angry, or upset by something said or done; to commit a crime.
▪ It offends me that you would make such a crass comment about my hair.
(Synonym) Affront, Insult, Transgress.

Officious (adjective) Used to describe an annoying person who tries to tell other people what to do in a way that is not wanted or needed; volunteering one's services where they are neither asked for nor needed; meddlesome.
▪ Catherine is an officious coworker, always butting in to tell us what we should do.
(Synonym) Bossy, Bureaucratic, Interfering.

Ominous (adjective) Suggesting that something bad is going to happen in the future.
▪ An ominous weather forecast promised a powerful storm.
(Synonym) Warning, Gloomy, Menacing. (Antonym) Promising.

Omniscient (adjective) Knowing everything; having unlimited understanding or knowledge.
▪ God is omniscient and omnipresent; he is all knowing and all powerful.
(Synonym) Wise, Sagacious, Well-informed.

Opaque (adjective) Blocking the passage or radiant energy and light; not transparent; difficult to understand or explain.
▪ Last summer, I swam in the opaque water of the muddy pool.
(Synonym) Cloudy, Obscure, Dense. (Antonym) Transparent.

Optimism (noun) A feeling or belief that good things will happen in the future; positive thoughts.
▪ I am optimistic about the future of renewable energy.
(Synonym) Hopefulness, Brightness, Enthusiasm. (Antonym) Pessimism.

Optimum (noun) The best or most advantageous condition; most effective.

- We mixed in oranges, lemons, and sugar for an optimum level of sweetness.
(Synonym) Finest, Optimal, Ideal. (Antonym) Worst.

Optional (adjective) Available as a choice but not required.
- At certain museums, students can get in free of charge but are asked for an optional donation.
(Synonym) Elective, Voluntary; Uncompelled. (Antonym) Compulsory.

Opulent (adjective) Very comfortable and expensive; luxurious; having a large estate or property; very wealthy.
- Gail bought an opulent new home near the river.
(Synonym) Wealthy, Lavish, Abundant. (Antonym) Poor.

Orator (noun) A person who makes speeches and is very good at making them; one distinguished for skill and power as an eloquent public speaker.
- Daniel Webster was an excellent and popular orator.
(Synonym) Lecturer, Debater, Narrator.

Orbit (verb) To travel around in a curved path; one complete circle around an object.
- Earth orbits the sun, and the moon orbits Earth.
(Synonym) Circle, Move around, Revolve.

Order (noun) An instruction or direction that must be obeyed; to put in order; arrange.
- Failing to obey an order from your superior is insubordination.
Out of order, not working properly; not able to be used.
- The elevator is out of order; you will need to use the stairs.
(Synonym) Command, Directive, Decree. (Antonym) Suggestion.

Ordinance (noun) A law or regulation made by a city or town government.
- Drinking in the park is prohibited by local ordinance.
(Synonym) Order, Rule, Decree.

Ostentatious (adjective) Displaying wealth or knowledge in a way that is meant to attract attention, admiration, or envy; pretentious display.
- Elizabeth makes sure that everyone is aware of her wealth; she spends lavishly and ostentatiously.
(Synonym) Boastful, Grandiose, Flashy. (Antonym) Modest.

Ostracize (verb) To exclude from a group by common consent; to exile by ostracism.
- The girls in middle school ostracized her; they did not include her in their social group.
(Synonym) Shun, Banish, Ignore. (Antonym) Include.

Ottoman (noun) A low piece of furniture with a soft top that you can put your feet on when you are sitting; a soft footstool.
- I sat on the ottoman because all the other seats were occupied.
(Synonym) Divan, Seat, Couch.

Ovation (noun) An occurrence in which a group of people show enthusiastic applause, by clapping their hands for a long period of time.
▪ The singer sang so beautifully that at the end of the performance she received a standing ovation.
(Synonym) Cheer, Acclaim, Prolonged applause.

Overthrow (verb) To remove from power, especially by force; bring down; defeat.
▪ The dictator was overthrown by a coup d'état.
(Synonym) Conquer, Defeat, Upheaval. (Antonym) Uphold.

Pacifist (noun) Someone who believes that war and violence are wrong and who refuses to support war.
▪ The pacifists suggested that we should have never started the war.
(Synonym) Peacekeeper, Peacemaker.

Paltry (adjective) Very small in amount; having little meaning, importance, or worth.
▪ His allowance was a paltry five dollars per week.
(Synonym) Insignificant, Meager, Miserable. (Antonym) Substantial.

Paradox (noun) A situation, person, or thing that combines contradictory features or qualities.
▪ The author George Orwell is known for this paradox: "All animals are created equal, but some are more equal than others."
(Synonym) Inconsistency, Contradiction, Enigma.

Parch (verb) To make something very dry or scorched.
▪ This year there was no harvest because the hot sun had parched the corn.
(Synonym) Burn, Dehydrate, Desiccate.

Parsimonious (adjective) Very unwilling to spend money; frugal to the point of stinginess.
▪ The company was so parsimonious this year that we did not have a holiday party.
(Synonym) Miserly, Sparing, Thrifty. (Antonym) Extravagant.

Partake (verb) To take part in something; to have a share along with others; participate in.
▪ I will partake in the fundraising effort for the children's sports scholarships.
(Synonym) Contribute, Assist, Involve. (Antonym) Refrain.

Peculiar (adjective) Not usual or normal; strange; not well; somewhat ill.
▪ It is peculiar that my daughter did not call for three days.
(Synonym) Odd, Weird, Unique. (Antonym) Normal.

Peddle (verb) To sell in small amounts, often by traveling from place to place.
▪ My ten-year-old sister peddles Girl Scout cookies to all the neighbors.
(Synonym) Promote, Market, Retail.

Pedometer (noun) An instrument that measures and registers the approximate distance one travels on foot.
- My pedometer indicated that I walked five miles at work yesterday.

Peer (noun) A person who belongs to the same age or social group as someone else; one of equal status with another.
- My son is loved and admired by his peers.
(Synonym) Colleague, Contemporary, Friend.

Pensive (adjective) Quietly sad or thoughtful.
- She is always daydreaming with a sad and pensive look on her face.
(Synonym) Meditative, Thinking, Reflective.

Penultimate (adjective) Occurring immediately before the last one; next to last.
- I am almost done reading the book; I just started the penultimate chapter.
(Synonym) Last but one, Second to last, One before the last.

Per capita (adverb) Equally to each individual; per unit of population.
- The country is so poor that the average annual per capita income is $200.
(Synonym) For each person, Per person, Per head.

Perceptive (adjective) Having the ability to understand or notice something easily or quickly.
- She is a very perceptive young woman; she makes acute observations.
(Synonym) Discerning, Aware, Observant.

Perilous (adjective) Full of danger, peril.
- The sport of mountain climbing entails a perilous journey before one finally reaches the summit.
(Synonym) Dangerous, Hazardous, Risky. (Antonym) Safe.

Permanent (adjective) Lasting or continuing for a very long time or forever; stable.
- A tattoo is a permanent addition to your skin; it is very difficult to erase.
(Synonym) Perpetual, Everlasting, Indelible. (Antonym) Temporary.

Permeable (adjective) Having pores or openings that allow liquids or gases to pass through; penetrable.
- The cell has a permeable membrane.
(Synonym) Leaky, Penetrable, Absorbent.

Pernicious (adjective) Causing great harm or damage, often in a way that is not easily seen or noticed; injurious; very harmful or destructive.
- Watching too much television and playing video games has a pernicious effect on childhood development.
(Synonym) Malicious, Wicked, Malignant. (Antonym) Harmless.

Perpetuity (noun) The state of continuing forever; eternity.
- If your portrait is enshrined in a museum, an image of your face will live on in perpetuity.
(Synonym) Endlessness, Infinity, Permanence.

Persevere (verb) To persist in an idea, purpose, or task despite obstacles.
- Despite all the difficulties she encountered, Amanda persevered and graduated summa cum laude from college.
(Synonym) Insist, Endure, Stick with.

Persistent (adjective) Continuing to do something even though it is difficult; not stopping.
- He has been persistent in his quest to find a cure for cancer.
(Synonym) Tenacious, Determined, Tireless. (Antonym) Irresolute.

Pertinent (adjective) Relating to the thing that is being thought about or discussed; relevant.
- "Is this war pertinent? Will it be on the test?" inquired Jane in her US history class.
(Synonym) Related, Applicable, Significant. (Antonym) Irrelevant.

Peruse (verb) To look or read in a relaxed way.
- This afternoon, I will go to the library and peruse the section on culinary books.
(Synonym) Scrutinize, Examine, Inspect.

Pessimistic (adjective) A lack of hope for the future; expecting bad things to happen; gloomy.
- There is no need to be pessimistic about the future; always try to look at the bright side of events.
(Synonym) Negative, Doubtful, Despondent. (Antonym) Optimistic.

Petty (adjective) Not very important or serious; having secondary rank or importance.
- Let us not waste time arguing over petty details.
(Synonym) Trivial, Small, Irrelevant. (Antonym) Important.

Philanthropic (adjective) Of a person or organization seeking to promote the welfare of others, by donating money or time to good causes.
- The school relies on philanthropic support to keep the music program running.
(Synonym) Benevolent, Humanitarian, Altruistic. (Antonym) Misanthropic.

Phobia (noun) An extremely strong and illogical fear.
- My fear of heights has developed into a full-blown phobia.
(Synonym) Dread, Paranoia, Anxiety.

Pied (adjective) Having two colors or more; patchy in color; multicolored; piebald.
- The Pied Piper, legendary kidnapper of children, wore a distinctive, multicolored outfit.
(Synonym) Multicolored, Variegated, Piebald. (Antonym) Plain.

Piety (noun) Devotion to God; the quality or state of being pious.
- She was admired for her extreme piety; she went to church several times a week.
(Synonym) Reverence, Virtue, Faith.

Placate (verb) To feel less angry; to soothe or mollify by yielding concessions; appease.
- My daughter was not placated by the gifts I bought her after I lost her teddy bear.
(Synonym) Calm, Conciliate, Satisfy. (Antonym) Enrage.

Placid (adjective) Not easily upset or excited; not moving much; calm and steady.
- The surface of the lake was placid, unruffled by even a breeze.
(Synonym) Docile, Serene, Quiet. (Antonym) Excitable.

Plagiarize (verb) To use the words or ideas of another person as if they were your own without attributing them to their original author.
- Do not plagiarize in your writing; it is against the honor code.
(Synonym) Copy, Steal, Imitate. (Antonym) Originate.

Plausible (adjective) Possibly true; believable or realistic.
- I think it is plausible that she could become the first woman to win the presidential election.
(Synonym) Reasonable, Credible, Probable.

Plea (noun) A serious and emotional request for something.
- At school, his mother made a dramatic plea to cancel the suspension of her son.
(Synonym) Petition, Request, Appeal.

Plead (verb) To make an emotional request; to make a plea or conduct pleadings in a cause or proceeding in a court.
- They encouraged him to plead the Fifth.
(Synonym) Implore, Beg, Importune.

Plethora (noun) A very large amount that is much greater than what is necessary; an excess.
- I have a plethora of information on college applications.
(Synonym) Overabundance, Glut, Surplus. (Antonym) Shortage.

Pliant (adjective) Able to bend without breaking; flexible; too easily influenced or controlled by other people.
- Andrew's behavior is pliant in nature; you can convince him to believe anything without much effort.
(Synonym) Docile, Malleable, Compliant. (Antonym) Rebellious.

Poise (noun) A calm, confident manner; a graceful way of walking, moving, standing.
- She read her speech with poise and grace.
(Synonym) Composure, Dignity, Self-possession.

Poisonous (adjective) Very harmful or unpleasant; causing sickness or death by entering or touching the body.
- Cyanide and bleach are poisonous chemicals.
(Synonym) Deadly, Malicious, Toxic.

Poll (noun) An activity in which many people are asked questions in order to get information about what most people think about something.
▪ The poll revealed that he is the favored candidate to win the next election.
(Synonym) Census, Survey, Referendum.

Pompous (adjective) Attitude of people who speak and behave in a very formal and serious way because they believe that they are better, smarter, or more important than other people.
▪ Emilie sounded pompous when she talked about attending the best college in Europe.
(Synonym) Ostentatious, Haughty, Pretentious. (Antonym) Modest.

Ponder (verb) To think about; to reflect on carefully and deeply.
▪ I pondered whether I could afford a trip to Dubai for Christmas.
(Synonym) Consider, Contemplate, Meditate upon.

Popular (adjective) Widely liked or enjoyed by many people.
▪ This song is very popular among teenagers.
(Synonym) Current, Common, Accepted. (Antonym) Rare.

Porous (adjective) Having small holes that allow air or liquid to pass through; permeable to fluids.
▪ The filter contained a porous membrane.
(Synonym) Absorbent, Leaky, Spongy. (Antonym) Impermeable.

Portable (adjective) Easy to carry or move around; able to be carried.
▪ He packed a portable DVD player in his bag.
(Synonym) Handy, Movable, Convenient. (Antonym) Fixed.

Portal (noun) A large door or gate to a building such as a church; a grand and imposing door.
▪ A time portal is said to be a gateway to another dimension.
(Synonym) Gateway, Doorway, Entrance.

Portentous (adjective) Extraordinary; marked by pompousness; giving a sign that something usually bad or unpleasant is going to happen.
▪ Last night, I had a portentous dream warning me of an imminent disaster.
(Synonym) Significant, Important, Ominous. (Antonym) Trivial.

Posthumous (adjective) Happening, done, or published after someone's death.
▪ The general received a posthumous award for his life of public service.
(Synonym) Subsequent, Following, Postmortem.

Postpone (verb) To put off to a later time; defer.
▪ The tennis game was postponed to tomorrow because of rain.
(Synonym) Delay, Reschedule, Adjourn. (Antonym) Continue.

Practical (adjective) Suited for actual use; having great usefulness; relating to what is real rather than to what is possible or imagined.
- She has a practical way of learning math problems.
(Synonym) Useful, Applied, Concrete. (Antonym) Theoretical.

Pragmatist (noun) A reasonable and logical way of doing things or thinking about problems that is based on dealing with specific situations instead of ideas and theories.
- Louise is a pragmatist; she always carefully considers her options and picks the most logical choice.
(Synonym) Realist, Rationalist, Practical person. (Antonym) Idealist.

Praise (verb) To express approval of or admiration for.
- The dance teacher praises the students who dance well to encourage them.
(Synonym) Acclaim, Commend, Applaud. (Antonym) Criticize.

Prance (verb) To walk or move in a lively and proud way; to move in high springy steps.
- The dancer pranced with effortless movements.
(Synonym) Swagger, Strut, Parade.

Preamble (noun) A statement that is made at the beginning of; an introductory statement.
- The students memorized the preamble to the US Constitution.
(Synonym) Foreword, Preface, Prelude. (Antonym) Postscript.

Precede (verb) To happen or come before; to be earlier than.
- President George W. Bush preceded President Barack H. Obama.
To surpass in rank, dignity, or importance; to do or say something before.
- The family tradition asks that a long prayer precede Thanksgiving dinner.
(Synonym) Head, Lead, Herald. (Antonym) Follow.

Predatory (adjective) Living by killing and eating other animals.
- Alligators are predatory animals.
Wrongly exploit others for personal profit.
- Some credit card companies practice predatory lending practices on consumers.
(Synonym) Greedy, Destructive, Carnivorous.

Predicament (noun) A difficult or unpleasant situation.
- I don't know how I ended up in this predicament; I can't pay the bills or buy food for my family.
(Synonym) Difficulty, Quandary, Dilemma.

Prediction (noun) A statement about what will happen or might happen in the future.
- The pundits have started making predictions about the winner of the upcoming election.
(Synonym) Prophecy, Expectation, Forecast.

Predilection (noun) A natural or habitual preference; a natural liking for something.
- I like studying in the library; it is my place of predilection.

(Synonym) Fondness, Penchant, Weakness. (Antonym) Dislike.

Preempt (verb) To take for oneself before others; to prevent something from happening.
- The security measures preempt fraud from happening.

To be shown instead of a scheduled television program, for example.
- The coverage of the presidential election preempted the weekly sitcom.

(Synonym) Anticipate, Obstruct, Appropriate.

Preface (noun) The introductory remarks of a speaker or author.
- In the preface of the book, the author thanked all those who had helped her in the process of writing it.

(Synonym) Foreword, Preamble, Prologue. (Antonym) Postscript.

Prehensile (adjective) Capable of grabbing or holding something by wrapping around it.
- Elephants use their prehensile trunks to grasp objects.

Prejudice (noun) An unfair feeling of dislike for a person or group because of race, sex, or religion, especially when it is not reasonable or logical.
- Martin Luther King Jr. fought against racial prejudice.

(Synonym) Bias, Discrimination, Intolerance. (Antonym) Impartiality.

Premonition (noun) A feeling or belief that something is going to happen when there is no definite reason to believe it will.
- I had a premonition that it was going to flood.

(Synonym) Forewarning, Feeling, Intuition.

Prerogative (noun) A right or privilege.
- It is the manager's prerogative to decide if the employees can leave early.

One belonging to a person, group, or class of individuals; a distinctive excellence.
- Education was once the prerogative of only the wealthy.

(Synonym) Choice, Entitlement, Birthright.

Preserve (verb) To keep something in its original state or in good condition; maintain.
- The community gathered to preserve the city's historical landmark.

To keep something safe from injury, harm, or destruction; protect.

(Synonym) Conserve, Maintain, Save.

Pretext (noun) A reason one gives to hide his or her real reason for doing something; pretense.
- Though they were really searching for drugs, the police stopped the cab under the pretext that the car's taillight was out.

(Synonym) Excuse, Cause, Ploy.

Prevail (verb) To defeat an opponent, especially in a long or difficult contest; gain ascendancy through strength or superiority; triumph.
- Good will always prevail over evil.

To be or continue to be in use; popular.

- At my children's school, mutual respect is the prevailing sentiment among students and teachers.

(Synonym) Succeed, Conquer, Triumph. (Antonym) Fail.

Prevalent (adjective) Accepted, done, or happening often or over a large area at a particular time; common or widespread.
- Montessori teaching methods are prevalent at many preparatory schools.

(Synonym) Predominant, Established, Dominant. (Antonym) Rare.

Primitive (adjective) Of, belonging to, or seeming to come from an earlier time.
- My Windows 2000 computer looks relatively primitive compared to recent advances in technology.

Not having a written language; produced by a people or culture that is nonindustrial and often non literate and tribal.
- Primitive cultures are found to have complex social systems.

(Synonym) Original, Basic, Prehistoric. (Antonym) Developed.

Principle (noun) A moral rule or belief that helps one know what is right and wrong and that influences one's actions; with respect to fundamentals.
- Blake always stood up for his principles; he did the right thing even when his choices were not popular.

(Synonym) Code, Norm, Standard.

Prior (adjective) Existing earlier in time; previous.
- Prior to working for the school library, I worked at Barnes & Noble bookstore.

(Synonym) Past, Preceding, Former. (Antonym) Subsequent.

Proclaim (verb) To announce or declare publicly or officially.
- Joshua Abraham Norton took command of the government and proclaimed himself emperor in 1859.

(Synonym) Pronounce, Make known , Say publicly.

Proclivity (noun) A tendency to do something that is usually bad.
- Why do some people have a proclivity for cruelty?

(Synonym) Penchant, Inclination, Propensity.

Procrastinate (verb) To be slow or late about doing something that should be done; to delay doing something until a later time because you do not want to do it.
- I am traveling to Prague this week; I do not want to procrastinate and leave my packing until the night before.

(Synonym) Postpone, Adjourn, Defer.

Prodigal (adjective) Carelessly and foolishly spending money, or time; characterized by profuse or wasteful expenditure; lavish.
- John left with all his father's money; he's a prodigal spender.

A child who leaves his or her parents to do things that they do not approve of but then feels sorry and returns home—often used figuratively.
▪ Joyce left her parents' house several months ago, but now the prodigal daughter has returned.
(Synonym) Immoderate, Reckless, Extravagant. (Antonym) Cautious.

Profane (adjective) Showing disrespect for religious things; to treat something sacred with irreverence; not religious or spiritual, secular.
▪ If you take the Lord's name in vain, you have profaned him.
(Synonym) Blasphemous, Irreverent, Disrespectful. (Antonym) Pious, Sacred.

Proficient (adjective) Good at doing something; well advanced in an art, occupation, or a branch of knowledge.
▪ My friend has become very proficient at playing video games.
(Synonym) Capable, Talented, Adept. (Antonym) Incompetent.

Profound (adjective) Having great knowledge or understanding; absolute or complete.
▪ Anne had profound insights in her last paper; I gave her an A because of her complete understanding of the subject material.
(Synonym) Intense, Deep, Insightful. (Antonym) Superficial.

Prognosis (noun) A doctor's opinion about how someone will recover from an illness or injury; forecast.
▪ When my father was sick, the doctor's prognosis was not good.
(Synonym) Projection, Diagnosis, Prospects.

Prohibit (verb) To prevent from doing something; to forbid by authority.
▪ Smoking is prohibited in all public places.
(Synonym) Interdict, Ban, Exclude. (Antonym) Permit.

Proletariat (noun) The lowest social or economic class of a community, especially the working class.
▪ The members of the proletariat demonstrated for the creation of a labor union.
(Synonym) Public, Grassroots, Blue-collar workers. (Antonym) Aristocracy.

Prolific (adjective) Abundantly productive.
▪ Joyce Carol Oates is one of the most prolific authors of our time; she has written more than one hundred books.
(Synonym) Fecund, Creative, Fertile.

Prologue (noun) An introduction to a book or play; the preface or introduction to a literary work.
▪ The play's prologue set the stage nicely.
Often used figuratively to denote an introductory or preceding event or development.
▪ The arrests were a prologue to widespread violence in the streets.
(Synonym) Prelude, Foreword, Preamble. (Antonym) Finale.

Prolong (verb) To make something last or continue for a longer time; to lengthen in time or scope.
▪ It's getting late, and I don't want to prolong this discussion on religion.
(Synonym) Extend, Delay, Elongate. (Antonym) Curtail.

Prominent (adjective) Important; widely and popularly well known.
▪ Oprah Winfrey is a reputable, prominent figure in the social media.
(Synonym) Outstanding, Noticeable, Conspicuous.

Promote (verb) To change the rank or position to a higher or more important one.
▪ The assistant teacher was promoted to the position of dean of students.
To contribute to the growth or prosperity of; further; to help develop or increase.
▪ The first lady promotes fitness for young people in schools throughout the country.
(Synonym) Endorse, Encourage, Advocate. (Antonym) Demote.

Prompt (verb) To cause someone to do something; to move to action; incite.
▪ My grandfather prompted me to join the military.
To show a message that tells a user to do something.
▪ The computer program prompted me to type my password.
Prompt (adjective) Arriving or doing something at the expected time or without delay.
▪ My coworker never misses a meeting and is always prompt.
(Synonym) Encourage, Provoke, Punctual.

Propaganda (noun) The spreading of ideas, information, or rumor for the purpose of helping or injuring an institution, a cause, or a person; ideas or statements that are often false or exaggerated and that are spread in order to help a cause, a political leader, or a government.
▪ Some magazines are spreading lies and propaganda about the union.
(Synonym) Publicity, Advertising, Misinformation.

Propel (verb) To push or drive someone or something forward or in a particular direction.
▪ At a stoplight, another car hit mine and propelled it into the intersection.
(Synonym) Force, Boost, Project.

Propensity (noun) A strong natural tendency to do something; intense natural inclination or preference.
▪ He has a propensity for violence and crime.
(Synonym) Predilection, Proclivity, Penchant.

Propose (verb) To suggest something, such as a plan or theory, to a person or group of people to consider.
▪ Beth proposed a petition calling for an end to unhealthy snacks.
(Synonym) Recommend, Suggest, Advise.

Prosper (verb) To become very successful usually by making a lot of money; to become very active, healthy, or strong and flourishing; to cause to succeed or thrive.

- My friend prospered as an ice cream vendor.
(Synonym) Flourish, Thrive, Succeed. (Antonym) Decline.

Protagonist (noun) A leading actor; the principal character in a novel, play, or movie; an important person who is involved in a competition, conflict, or cause.
- Jay Gatsby was the protagonist In *The Great Gatsby*.
(Synonym) Character, Hero, Leading role.

Prowl (verb) To move through a place while searching for something, often in a quiet or secret way.
- The police prowled the street hoping to catch the criminal.
(Synonym) Stalk, Scavenge, Sneak.

Prune (noun) A dried plum that is often cooked before it is eaten.
- My grandfather drank a glass of prune juice every morning.

Prune (verb) To cut off some of the branches of a tree or bush so that it will grow or look better.
- Every year we prune the bushes in front of our house.
(Synonym) Trim, Reduce, Curtail.

QUIZ 9- MATCH EACH WORD IN THE FIRST COLUMN WITH ITS SYNONYM IN THE SECOND COLUMN. CHECK YOUR ANSWERS IN THE BACK OF THE BOOK.

1. neophyte	a. dangerous
2. nocturnal	b. sell
3. noxious	c. thrive
4. obdurate	d. forbid
5. obsolete	e. contradiction
6. obvious	f. excess
7. ovation	g. novice
8. paradox	h. stubborn
9. peddle	i. old-fashioned
10. perilous	j. apparent
11. peruse	k. by night
12. phobia	l. read
13. plethora	m. fear
14. prohibit	n. harmful
15. prosper	o. applause

Punctual (adjective) Arriving at the expected or planned time; being on time; prompt.
- The students are always punctual but their professor is often tardy.
(Synonym) On time, Prompt, In good time. (Antonym) Late.

Purge (verb) To remove; to cause something to leave the body.
- The doctor prescribed a medication to purge my digestive system before my colonoscopy.
(Synonym) Eliminate, Clear, Get rid of.

Purist (noun) The quality or state of being pure; a person who has very strong ideas about what is correct or acceptable and who usually opposes changes to traditional methods and practices.
- He is a purist of the French language.
(Synonym) Traditionalist, Pedant, Perfectionist. (Antonym) Radical.

Quadrant (noun) One part of something that is evenly divided into four parts; a quarter.
- The two intersecting lines divide the circle into four quadrants.

Quagmire (noun) An area of soft, wet ground.
- The city was once a quagmire of muddy flats.
A situation that is hard to deal with or get out of; a situation that is full of problems.
- I am caught in a quagmire with all my homework that I left until the last minute.
(Synonym) Swamp, Dilemma, Sticky situation.

Quandary (noun) A situation in which one is confused about what to do.
- For her prom, Miriam was in a quandary about which dress to wear.
(Synonym) Dilemma, Quagmire, Puzzlement.

Quarantine (noun) The period of time during which a person with a disease is kept away from others.
- Long ago, people diagnosed with tuberculosis were put into quarantine.
(Synonym) Isolation, Seclusion, Separation.

Quell (verb) To end or stop something by using force; to calm or reduce fear.
- I drank some cold water and took deep breaths in order to quell my anxiety before the exam.
(Synonym) Suppress, Put down, Stifle. (Antonym) Incite.

Quench (verb) To stop a fire from burning; to put out a fire.
- Firefighters quenched the flames in the building.
To cause someone to stop feeling thirsty; to relieve or satisfy with liquid.
- A small bottle of juice will quench my thirst for the day.
(Synonym) Suppress, Satisfy, Control.

Query (noun) A question or a request for information about something.
- The admission office representative responded to all my queries about my college
  application.
(Synonym) Inquiry, Interrogation, Question. (Antonym) Certainty.

Radiate (verb) To proceed in a direct line from or toward a center. To send out rays; shine brightly.
- The sun radiates light and warmth.
(Synonym) Emit, Discharge, Shine.

Ransack (verb) To search a place for something in a way that causes disorder or damage; search thoroughly.
- The burglars ransacked the apartment and left nothing behind.
(Synonym) Vandalize, Loot, Pillage.

Ratify (verb) To make a treaty or agreement official by signing it or voting for it.
- The state legislatures must ratify an amendment to the US Constitution.
(Synonym) Endorse, Approve, Authorize.

Rational (adjective) Having the ability to reason or think about things clearly based on facts and not on emotions or feelings; understanding.
- Humans are rational beings.
(Synonym) Normal, Coherent, Logical.

Ravenous (adjective) Very hungry; very eager or greedy for food.
- After playing basketball for many hours, I was ravenous for dinner.
(Synonym) Gluttonous, Voracious, Insatiable. (Antonym) Sated.

Raze (verb) To destroy completely, such as a building; demolish.
- The old factory was razed to make room for a parking lot.
(Synonym) Devastate, Annihilate, Tear Down. (Antonym) Build.

Reaction (noun) The way someone acts or feels in response to something that is said or happens.
- I could see by my friend's reaction that he was sad when I told him I was moving to Europe next year.
(Synonym) Feedback, Effect, Answer.

Reality (noun) The true situation that exists; the real situation.
- Aaron refused to face the reality that death exists.
(Synonym) Authenticity, Fact, Certainty. (Antonym) Idealism.

Recalcitrant (adjective) Stubbornly refusing to obey rules or orders; difficult to manage or operate; not responsive to treatment; resistant.
- Recalcitrant Democrats and Republicans are loyal to their political parties and unwilling to compromise.
(Synonym) Unruly, Refractory, Disobedient. (Antonym) Cooperative.

Recession (noun) A period of time when there is a decrease in economic activity and many people do not have jobs.
- Many people lost their jobs during the recent recession.

The act of moving back or away slowly; the act of receding.
(Synonym) Downturn, Decline, Stagnation. (Antonym) Boom.

Recessive (adjective) A characteristic or condition that a child will have only if both of the child's parents have it.
▪ Recessive genes were responsible for his blue eyes.
(Synonym) Receding, Retreating, Dormant. (Antonym) Dominant.

Recluse (noun) A person who lives alone and avoids other people.
▪ A lot of students recluse themselves during exam time.
(Synonym) Solitary, Hermit, Loner.

Recollect (verb) To remember something.
▪ Because it has been several years since I took Latin, I struggle to recollect Roman proverbs.
(Synonym) Recall, Reminisce, Remember.

Reconciliation (noun) The act of causing two people or groups to become friendly again after an argument.
▪ A month after a brutal argument, Andrew and Josh finally attempted a reconciliation.
(Synonym) Compromise, Understanding, Resolution. (Antonym) Conflict.

Rectify (verb) To correct something that is wrong; to set right; remedy.
▪ The company management promised to rectify the problem with the component.
(Synonym) Resolve, Fix, Adjust. (Antonym) Damage.

Redeem (verb) To make something that is bad or unpleasant better or more acceptable.
▪ After being irritable with my grandmother, I redeemed myself by bringing her flowers and apologizing.
To exchange something, such as a coupon or lottery ticket, for money or an award.
▪ My parents always redeem the 20 percent off coupon at the supermarket.
To do something good after you have failed or done something bad; to save people from sin and evil.
▪ Christians believe that Jesus Christ was sent to Earth to redeem us from sin.
(Synonym) Cash, Exchange, Convert. (Antonym) Keep.

Redundant (adjective) Using more words than necessary; characterized by similarity or repetition; laid off from a job because you are no longer needed; containing an excess.
▪ My mentor edited my essay and removed all redundant phrases.
(Synonym) Unnecessary, Superfluous, Surplus.

Refractory (adjective) Difficult to treat or cure; unresponsive to stimulus; resisting control or authority.
▪ Some cases of anemia are classified as a refractory disease.
(Synonym) Headstrong, Stubborn, Disobedient. (Antonym) Placid.

Refuge (noun) A place that provides shelter or protection from danger, trouble, or

distress; something to which one has recourse in difficulty.
- I have found refuge from the modern world in classical music.
(Synonym) Sanctuary, Shelter, Protection.

Refute (verb) To say or prove that something is not true.
- John refuted the claims of the teacher who said he was talking in class.
(Synonym) Disprove, Contradict, Repudiate. (Antonym) Prove.

Regretful (adjective) Feeling or showing regret.
- He made a regretful decision that he must now live with for the rest of his life.
(Synonym) Remorseful, Contrite, Sorry.

Reimburse (verb) To pay someone an amount of money equal to an amount that the person has spent.
- My employer reimbursed me for school tuition.
(Synonym) Repay, Refund, Compensate.

Relinquish (verb) To give up power, control, or possession to another person or group; to withdraw or retreat from; to leave behind.
- Malia was forced to relinquish control of the construction project.
(Synonym) Surrender, Abandon, Resign. (Antonym) Retain.

Relish (verb) Enjoyment of or delight in something that satisfies one's tastes, inclinations, or desires.
- He devoured two pieces of pumpkin pie with great relish.
(Synonym) Like, Enjoy, Appreciate. (Antonym) Dislike.

Reluctant (adjective) Feeling or showing doubt about doing something; not willing or eager to do something.
- We were reluctant to participate in the protest.
(Synonym) Unwilling, Hesitant, Averse. (Antonym) Enthusiastic, Keen.

Remorse (noun) A feeling of being sorry for doing something bad or wrong in the past; a feeling of guilt.
- He did not express remorse after killing his fiancée.
(Synonym) Sorrow, Repentance, Guilt.

Remunerate (verb) To pay an equivalent to for a service, loss, or expense; recompense.
- John will be remunerated for finding the dog.
(Synonym) Reward, Compensate, Reimburse.

Renaissance (noun) The period of European history between the fourteenth and seventeenth centuries when there was a new interest in science, ancient art, and literature, especially in Italy; a period of new growth or activity.
- I bought a catalog on the art and architecture of the Renaissance.
(Synonym) Rebirth, Revival, New beginning. (Antonym) Decline.

Repress (verb) To not allow yourself to do or express something; to hold in by self-control; to prevent the natural or normal expression, activity, or development of.
▪ She repressed a laugh while her cousin was delivering a speech.
To not allow yourself to remember something, such as an unpleasant event; to exclude from consciousness.
▪ I try to repress the painful memory of my aunt's death.
(Synonym) Prevent, Suppress, Inhibit. (Antonym) Express.

Reprimand (verb) To speak in an angry and critical way to someone who has done something wrong or disobeyed an order.
▪ My friends were reprimanded for being late to school.
(Synonym) Castigate, Chide, Scold. (Antonym) Praise.

Reprisal (noun) An act to hurt or punish someone who has hurt or done something bad to someone else.
▪ The witness asked to avoid using her real name on the blog for fear of reprisals.
(Synonym) Revenge, Retaliation, Payback.

Reproach (noun) An expression of disapproval or disappointment.
▪ She looked at him with an air of reproach.
(Synonym) Censure, Blame, Reprimand.

Repudiate (verb) To refuse to accept or support.
▪ The defense attorneys brought to light new evidence that repudiates the allegations.
(Synonym) Reject, Renounce, Deny.

Repugnant (adjective) Causing a strong feeling of dislike or disgust; exciting distaste or aversion.
▪ The kitchen's garbage bin gives off a repugnant smell.
(Synonym) Distasteful, Obscene, Offensive. (Antonym) Agreeable.

Reputable (adjective) Respected and trusted by most people; having a good reputation; held in esteem.
▪ The hospital hired a reputable and highly recommended surgeon.
(Synonym) Trustworthy, Honest, Upright.

Repute (noun) Being highly thought of; the state of being held in high esteem and honor.
▪ To keep his high repute, Ron never participated in irresponsible behaviors.
(Synonym) Fame, Renown, Status.

Require (verb) To need something; to demand as necessary or essential.
▪ The law requires that you attend school until you are sixteen years of age.
(Synonym) Oblige, Compel, Command.

Rescind (verb) To say officially that something is no longer valid; to end a law, contract, or agreement.

- I learned that the company decided to rescind the job offer.
(Synonym) Withdraw, Annul, Cancel. (Antonym) Reinstate, Validate.

Resilience (noun) The ability to become strong, healthy, or successful again after something bad happens; the ability to return to its original shape after it has been pulled, stretched, pressed, etc.
- The Haitian people showed remarkable resilience in dealing with the earthquake's effects.
(Synonym) Elasticity, Serenity, Strength.

Resolute (adjective) Very determined; having or showing a lot of determination; firm.
- Audrey is a strong and resolute competitor.
(Synonym) Determined, Stubborn, Definite. (Antonym) Hesitant.

Resolve (verb) To find an answer or solution to something; to make clear or understandable.
- The two countries finally resolved their conflict.
(Synonym) Solve, Agree, Determine.

Respite (noun) An interval of rest or relief; a short period of time when you are able to stop doing something that is difficult or unpleasant.
- The week of vacation provided a welcome respite from my hectic job.
(Synonym) Reprieve, Pause, Hiatus.

Restitution (noun) The act of returning something that was lost or stolen to its owner; payment that is made to someone for damage.
- Chelsea rejoiced when the police called her to give her the restitution of her stolen car—undamaged.
(Synonym) Compensation, Reimbursement, Restoration.

Retain (verb) To keep in possession or use.
- The company has to retain competent and dependable employees.
To keep something in your memory, especially for a long period of time.
- Victoria has a remarkable memory; she has the ability to retain the smallest details.
(Synonym) Recall, Hold on to, Recollect.

Retard (verb) To slow down the development or progress of something.
- Lack of funds has retarded the opening of the after-school program.
(Synonym) Delay, Keep back, Impede.

Reticent (adjective) Inclined to be silent or uncommunicative in speech; reserved.
- She is reticent about her past with her colleagues.
(Synonym) Discreet, Taciturn, Timid. (Antonym) Talkative.

Retribution (noun) Punishment for doing something wrong.
- The family is seeking retribution for the killing of their son.
(Synonym) Vengeance, Revenge, Reprisal.

Revere (verb) To have great respect for someone; regard as worthy of great honor.
▪ We revere peacemakers like Martin Luther King Jr. and Mahatma Gandhi.
(Synonym) Admire, Esteem, Venerate.

Reversal (noun) A change to an opposite state, condition, or decision.
▪ In a sudden reversal, the congressman voted for the act that he had opposed so
  vehemently for a year.
(Synonym) Inversion, Reverse, Turnaround.

Revise (verb) To make changes, especially to correct or improve something.
▪ This report has been revised to include additional details.
(Synonym) Adjust, Amend, Modify.

Revolve (verb) To turn around a center point or line.
▪ Earth revolves around the sun.
To have someone or something as a main subject or interest.
▪ The debate revolved around which student should be nominated the valedictorian of
  the graduating class.
(Synonym) Rotate, Consider, Gyrate.

Revulsion (noun) A sudden or a very strong feeling of dislike or disgust.
▪ She experienced shock and revulsion at the blatant abuse of human rights.
(Synonym) Repulsion, Distaste, Repugnance. (Antonym) Attraction.

Rickety (adjective) Not strong or stable and likely to break.
▪ My cousin is driving a rickety old car.
(Synonym) Shaky, Unbalanced, Feeble. (Antonym) Firm.

Rife (adjective) Very common in occurrence and often bad or unpleasant.
▪ Last summer, my sister visited Sierra Leone where Ebola was rife.
(Synonym) Predominant, Widespread, Endemic. (Antonym) Sparse.

Rigorous (adjective) Very strict and demanding; favoring rigor; scrupulously accurate; precise.
▪ The school curriculum is incredibly rigorous.
(Synonym) Severe, Arduous, Scrupulous. (Antonym) Mild.

Robust (adjective) Strong and healthy; having or exhibiting strength or vigorous health.
▪ My grandmother is in robust health even though she's in her late nineties.
(Synonym) Vigorous, Hearty, Forceful. (Antonym) Weak.

Root (noun) The part of a plant that grows underground and holds the plant in place;
the cause or source of something.
▪ The root of her difficulties in math was her inability to read what the problem asked.
(Synonym) Origin, Cause, Source.

Roster (noun) A list of names; a list of personnel available for duty.
- His name has been added to the basketball team's roster.
(Synonym) Schedule, Register, Timetable.

Rouse (verb) To wake someone from sleep; to cause an emotional response in someone.
- The mayor's comments roused the anger of the police.
(Synonym) Provoke, Incite, Awake.

Ruse (noun) A trick or act that is used to fool someone.
- John thought of a ruse in order to take some candy from his mom's cabinet.
(Synonym) Hoax , Maneuver, Scam.

Ruthless (adjective) Having no pity; cruel or merciless.
- The dictator was ruthless with his opponent.
(Synonym) Callous, Unsparing, Cold-blooded. (Antonym) Merciful.

Salutary (adjective) Producing a beneficial effect after something unpleasant has happened; remedial.
- The injury-free accident was a salutary reminder of the dangers of drinking and driving.
(Synonym) Helpful, Beneficial, Valuable.

Sanctuary (noun) A place where someone or something is protected or given shelter; a consecrated place.
- Her music room is her sanctuary from the pressure of the quotidian life.
(Synonym) Refuge, asylum, shelter.

Satiate (verb) To fully satisfy a need; the state of being fed or gratified to or beyond capacity.
- His hunger could never be fully satiated.
(Synonym) Satisfy, Fill, Quench.

Satisfy (verb) To cause to be happy or please; meet the expectations, needs, or desires of someone.
- She satisfied all the requirements needed to pass her driving test.
(Synonym) Content, Fulfill, Appease.

Saturate (verb) To soak completely; to make something very wet.
- The heavy rainstorm saturated the ground.
To satisfy fully; satiate; to load to capacity.
- Farmers have grown so much wheat this year that they have exceeded consumer demand, thus saturating the market and driving down prices.
(Synonym) Drench, Oversupply, Inundate. (Antonym) Dry out.

QUIZ 10.- MATCH EACH WORD IN THE FIRST COLUMN WITH ITS SYNONYM IN THE SECOND COLUMN. CHECK YOUR ANSWERS IN THE BACK OF THE BOOK.

1. quandary	a. revival
2. quench	b. widespread
3. radiate	c. stubborn
4. ransack	d. satisfy
5. ratify	e. trick
6. recollect	f. puzzlement
7. refractory	g. strict
8. redundant	h. search thoroughly
9. refuge	i. slow down
10. renaissance	j. shine
11. reputable	k. shelter
12. retard	l. superfluous
13. rife	m. approve
14. rigorous	n. remember
15. ruse	o. honest

Scarce (adjective) Very small in amount or number compared with the demand; not plentiful or abundant.
- I was working in a hospital in the developing world where medicine was unavailable and food was scarce.
(Synonym) Limited, Meager, Rare. (Antonym) Abundance.

Scavenge (verb) To search for food to eat; to search through waste or junk for something that can be saved or used.
- Gloria is very frugal; she is always scavenging at the flea market for clothes and shoes.
(Synonym) Hunt, Rummage, Forage.

Scold (verb) To speak in an angry or critical way to someone who has done something wrong.
- The teacher scolded the children for making too much noise.
(Synonym) Reprimand, Berate, Discipline.

Scrupulous (adjective) Careful in doing what is needed, honest, and morally right.
- Elizabeth is scrupulous when doing her homework; she pays a lot of attention to details.
(Synonym) Meticulous, Rigorous, Conscientious.

Scrutinize (verb) To examine carefully, closely, and minutely, especially in a critical way; close watch; surveillance.
- I scrutinized the purse before buying it to verify whether it was authentic.
(Synonym) Inspect, Investigate, Analyze.

Secure (adjective) Protected from danger or harm.
- The children were secure and safe in their home.
(Synonym) Sheltered, Assured, Safe.

Sedate (adjective) Keeping a quiet steady attitude or pace; slow and relaxed.
- On her wedding day, she walked sedately down the aisle.
(Synonym) Dignified, Calm, Serene.

Sedentary (adjective) Doing a lot of sitting; not physically active.
- Mary is a quintessential couch potato; she lives a sedentary life.
(Synonym) Inactive, Stationary, Deskbound. (Antonym) Active.

Seep (verb) To flow or pass slowly through small openings in something.
- Water was seeping through the roof.
(Synonym) Leak, Escape, Ooze.

Sentry (noun) A soldier who guards a certain place.
- The soldier was assigned to be the sentry at the outpost's front gate.
(Synonym) Patrol, Watch, Sentinel.

Serene (adjective) Being calm, quiet, and peaceful.
- She has a serene expression on her face.
(Synonym) Tranquil, Composed, Poised. (Antonym) Bustling.

Sermon (noun) A speech about a moral or religious subject that is usually given by a religious leader as a part of a worship service.
- The preacher gave an inspiring sermon on the power of hope.
(Synonym) Oration, Homily, Address.

Sever (verb) To cut off; to end a relationship completely.
- Her legs were severed in a car accident.
(Synonym) Divide, Separate, Split. (Antonym) Unite.

Severe (adjective) Very bad, serious or unpleasant; extreme.
- There have been severe storms on the East Coast.
(Synonym) Harsh, Brutal, Critical.

Shame (noun) A feeling of guilt, regret, embarrassment, or sadness because you know you have done something wrong.
- When she came out of jail, she never went out of her house; she lived with the shame of being arrested.
(Synonym) Disgrace, Humiliation, Dishonor. (Antonym) Pride.

Shield (noun) A large piece of metal carried by someone such as a soldier or police officer for protection; one that defends or protects.
▪ The bank robbers escaped police by using a customer as a human shield.
(Synonym) Defense, Safeguard, Protection. (Antonym) Expose.

Shrewd (adjective) Having an ability to understand and to make good judgments; mentally sharp or clever.
▪ Uncle Friedman is a shrewd businessman who always makes a profit.
(Synonym) Smart, Astute, Insightful.

Shrill (adjective) Having or emitting a very loud, sharp, high-pitched tone or sound; piercing.
▪ The shrill sound of the old steam locomotive's whistle woke me up.
(Synonym) Penetrating, Sharp, Harsh. (Antonym) Low.

Shroud (noun) A cloth that is used to wrap a dead body; something that covers or hides; burial garment.
▪ A shroud of secrecy enveloped the process of producing the drink.
(Synonym) Covering, Blanket, Veil.

Signify (verb) To be a sign of; to mean something; to have importance or to matter.
▪ In some cultures, black clothing signifies mourning.
To show your feelings, intentions, or opinions by doing something.
▪ My father nodded to signify his approval.
(Synonym) Mean, Indicate, Imply.

Similar (adjective) The same; having characteristics in common; alike in substance or essentials; corresponding.
▪ My friends and I have similar tastes in clothing.
(Synonym) Comparable, Equivalent, Analogous. (Antonym) Different.

Sincere (adjective) Genuine or real; having true feelings that are expressed in an honest way.
▪ Her joy about our achievements was sincere.
(Synonym) Heartfelt, Serious, Frank.

Sinister (adjective) Having an evil appearance; looking likely to cause something bad, harmful, or dangerous to happen.
▪ When I met him the first time, I felt something sinister about him.
(Synonym) Menacing, Threatening, Wicked.

Skeptic (noun) A person who often questions or doubts something such as a claim or statement.
▪ She became a skeptic about her chances of ever winning the lottery.
(Synonym) Cynic, Disbeliever, Questioner.

Slander (noun) A false spoken statement that causes people to have a bad opinion of someone.
- The man is being sued for slander because of the false characterizations he publicly uttered about his neighbor.
(Synonym) Insult, Defamation, libel.

Sluggish (adjective) Moving slowly or lazily.
- A sluggish economy led to the workers being laid off.
(Synonym) Lethargic, Inactive, listless. (Antonym) Lively.

Smite (verb) To hurt, kill, or punish; to hit something very hard.
- Hardship smote the family after they bought their house.
(Synonym) Smack, Strike, Slash.

Snuggle (verb) To lie or sit close together in a comfortable position; to curl up comfortably or cozily.
- The toddler snuggled with her parents at the airport.
(Synonym) Cuddle, Snug, Nuzzle.

Sober (adjective) Not drunk; having or showing a very serious attitude or quality.
- My father has been sober for twenty years.
Plain in color.
- She wore a sober gray dress.
(Synonym) Abstemious, Somber, Moderate.

Sojourn (noun) A period of time when you stay in a place as a traveler or guest; a temporary stay.
- Our family's sojourn at Wahoo Bay was a well-deserved respite from city life.
(Synonym) Vacation, Visit, Break.

Solace (noun) To give a feeling of comfort to a person who is sad, depressed, in grief, or has suffered misfortune.
- After the death of her parents, she found solace in her music.
(Synonym) Consolation, Relief, Succor. (Antonym) Aggravation.

Solicit (verb) To ask for something such as money or help from people.
- The organization is soliciting donations from celebrities to help victims of the earthquake.
(Synonym) Implore, Request, Petition.

Solitary (adjective) Isolated or done alone.
- Prisoners are sometimes punished by being placed in solitary confinement.
(Synonym) Single, Alone, Secluded.

Somnolent (adjective) Tired and ready to fall asleep; in a state between sleeping and waking.
- He was fired for being somnolent in the workplace.
(Synonym) Drowsy, Lethargic, Dozy.

Sparse (adjective) Present only in small amounts; less than necessary or normal.
- Furniture and decorations were sparse in her home.
(Synonym) Scarce, Thin, Meager.

Spectrum (noun) An entire range of light waves; the colors that can be seen in a rainbow; a complete range of different people or opinions.
- New York City's population is a broad spectrum of cultural backgrounds.
(Synonym) Variety, Gamut, Continuum.

Speculative (adjective) Based on guesses or ideas about what might happen or be true rather than on facts; assumption.
- Your ideas on the business venture are purely speculative.
(Synonym) Hypothetical, Theoretical, Projected. (Antonym) Proven.

Spontaneous (adjective) Done or said in a natural and sudden way without a lot of thought or planning.
- Elizabeth spontaneously offered a helping hand.
(Synonym) Spur of the moment, Impulsive, Unplanned.

Sporadic (adjective) Occurring occasionally, singly, or in irregular or random instances; not constant or steady.
- The passengers ran after hearing sporadic explosions near the airport.
(Synonym) Erratic, Intermittent, Random. (Antonym) Regular.

Spurious (adjective) Not genuine, sincere, or authentic; based on false ideas or bad reasoning.
- The politician was infamous for his spurious statements.
(Synonym) False, Counterfeit, Imitation.

Spurn (verb) To refuse to accept; to reject something disdainfully.
- She spurned the company's job offer and went to work for a competitor.
(Synonym) Scorn, Repulse, Despise. (Antonym) Accept.

Stagnant (adjective) Not flowing in a current stream; not active, advancing, or progressing.
- The stagnant economy led to a reduction in the company's workforce.
(Synonym) Sluggish, Inactive, Dormant.

Staid (adjective) Serious, boring, or old-fashioned.
- My great-aunt's staid demeanor alienated some of the young people.
(Synonym) Serious, Sedate, Dull. (Antonym) Exciting.

Stalemate (noun) A contest, dispute, or competition in which neither side can gain an advantage or win.
- The warring factions were locked in a stalemate with neither side able to advance.
(Synonym) Tie, Deadlock, Impasse.

Stall (verb) To stop suddenly because of a problem, especially to cause an engine to stop inadvertently; to stop flying suddenly and begin to fall because an aircraft's wings cannot produce enough lift.
- The car's engine stalled when he let out the clutch pedal too quickly.
(Synonym) Delay, Slowed down, Stop.

Stalwart (adjective) Marked by outstanding strength and vigor of body, mind, or spirit; very loyal and dedicated.
- My daughters are strong and stalwart.
(Synonym) Athletic, Brave, Hefty.

Stance (noun) A publicly stated opinion; a way of standing or being place; intellectual or emotional attitude.
- She took a firm stance on public education and voted to increase the school budget.
(Synonym) Attitude, Standpoint, Opinion.

Stanza (noun) Basic metrical unit in a poem , typically of four or more lines.
- He wrote the first stanza of a poem for today's English class.
(Synonym) Verse, Canto, Strophe.

Stare (verb) To look at someone or something for a long time often with your eyes wide open.
- The little girl was staring at Santa Claus near the Christmas tree in the mall.
To look directly into someone's eyes without fear until he or she becomes uncomfortable and looks away.
(Synonym) Gaze, Look intently, Watch. (Antonym) Glance.

Static (adjective) Showing little or no change, action, or progress; characterized by a lack of movement, animation, or progression.
- Culture is not static.
Of, relating to, or producing static electricity.
- Use a fabric softener when drying clothing to prevent static cling.
(Synonym) Inactive, Stagnant, Not moving.

Stationary (adjective) Not moving; staying in one place or position; unchanging in condition; fixed in a station, course, or mode; immobile.
- The car remained stationary despite Jack's attempts to get it rolling.
(Synonym) Motionless, At a halt, Fixed.

Steadfast (adjective) Very devoted or loyal to a person, belief, or cause; not changing.
- The United States and Canada are steadfast friends.
(Synonym) Persistent, Dedicated, Constant.

Stench (noun) A very bad smell, stink; a characteristic repugnant quality.
- I cannot take the stench of the garbage truck.
Sometimes used figuratively.

• The stench of corruption permeated the state capitol chambers.
(Synonym) Stink, disgusting odor, unpleasant smell. (Antonym) Perfume.

Sterile (adjective) Clean and free of bacteria and germs; incapable of producing crops, plants, fruit, or spores; incapable of producing offspring.
• The women were sterile after their accidental exposure to ionizing radiation.
(Synonym) Germ-free, Sanitary, Unproductive.

Sterling (adjective) Made of silver that is 92 percent pure.
• Nowadays, there is a rise in the value of sterling silver.
Very good, excellent.
• She came to the meeting with sterling ideas.
(Synonym) Genuine, Authentic, First-rate. (Antonym) Spurious.

Stern (adjective) Very serious, especially in an unfriendly way; having a definite hardness or severity of nature.
• The judge has a stern face.
To be an emotionally and morally strong person with more determination than other people.
• Another woman would have broken down, but Amenise is made of sterner stuff.
(Synonym) Austere, Strict, Firm.

Stimulate (verb) To make something more active; to cause or encourage something to happen or develop.
• In an effort to stimulate the economy, the government is creating new jobs.
(Synonym) Rouse, Give an incentive to, Encourage.

Stimulus (noun) To cause something else to happen, develop, or become more active.
• The government is encouraging economic activity by creating a stimulus package.
(Synonym) Incentive, Motivation, Incitement.

Stipulate (verb) To demand or require something as part of an agreement; to specify as a condition or requirement.
• The new rule of the school stipulates that players must wear uniforms.
(Synonym) Specify, Require, Demand.

Stoop (verb) To walk or stand with your head and shoulders bent forward.
• My brother is so tall that he has to stoop to get through the low doorways.
To descend from a superior rank, dignity, or status; to lower oneself morally; to do something that is not honest or fair.
• She would never stoop to the status of stealing food out of the fridge.
(Synonym) Condescend, Bend, Lower yourself.

Strenuous (adjective) Requiring or showing great energy and effort; vigorously active.
• Yesterday in the gym, I was exhausted by the strenuous workout.
(Synonym) Active, Tireless, Energetic. (Antonym) Light.

Strife (noun) Very angry or violent disagreement between groups; fight, struggle.
- Religious strife remains at the root of many armed conflicts.
(Synonym) Trouble, Conflict, Rivalry. (Antonym) Harmony.

Strike (verb) To hit someone or something in a forceful way; to come into contact forcefully.
- She was struck and killed by a car.
(Synonym) Raid, Attack, Assault.

Stringent (adjective) Very strict or severe.
- The guidelines for our English paper were stringent.
(Synonym) Rigorous, Rigid, Demanding. (Antonym) Lax, Flexible.

Stubborn (adjective) Refusing to change your ideas or to stop doing something; difficult to deal with.
- She is a stubborn child; her favorite word seems to be "no."
(Synonym) Persistent, Tenacious, Obstinate. (Antonym) Flexible.

Stymie (verb) To stop someone from doing something or to stop something from happening.
- Playing video games stymied students' effort to finish their homework.
To present an obstacle to; stand in the way of.
- Progress on the road's construction has been stymied by lack of money.
(Synonym) Frustrate, Hinder, Prevent. (Antonym) Encourage.

Submerge (verb) To cover or overflow with water; to go underwater.
- Our car in the parking lot was submerged in floodwater.
To make yourself fully involved in an activity or interest.
- After her graduation from medical school, she submerged herself in research in the hope of finding a cure for cancer.
(Synonym) Plunge, Immerse, Dip.

Submissive (adjective) Willing to obey someone else.
- The submissive man agreed to hand over his wallet to the weaponless mugger.
(Synonym) Obedient, Docile, Compliant.

Subsequent (adjective) Following in time, order, or place; happening or coming after something else.
- She left a legacy that will benefit subsequent generations.
(Synonym) Succeeding, Consequent, Later. (Antonym) Preceding.

Subservient (adjective) Very willing to obey someone else; useful in an inferior capacity; subordinate.
- In some cultures, women are expected to remain subservient.
(Synonym) Submissive, Obedient, Docile. (Antonym) Assertive.

Subversive (adjective) Secretly trying to ruin or destroy a government or political system.
▪ Advocating the overthrow of the government is a subversive activity.
(Synonym) Dissident, Insubordinate, Destructive.

Succinct (adjective) Using few words to state or express an idea; briefly expressed; terse.
▪ The mentor advised her to rewrite the essay in two succinct pages.
(Synonym) Concise, Brief, Direct. (Antonym) Wordy.

Succor (noun) Help that is given to someone who is suffering or in a difficult situation.
▪ The Red Cross provided succor to the survivors of the storm.
(Synonym) Relief, Comfort, Assistance.

Succumb (verb) To stop trying to resist something, to yield to superior strength or force.
▪ After a long fight, he succumbed to liver cancer.
(Synonym) Submit, Surrender, Capitulate.

Suffocate (verb) Cause to die from lack of air or inability to breathe.
▪ He swallowed a whole meatball, choked on it, and nearly suffocated.
(Synonym) Choke, Asphyxiate, Deprive of air.

Sullen (adjective) Used to describe an angry or unhappy person who does not want to talk.
▪ The podiatrist had a sullen expression on his face when he examined my feet.
(Synonym) Surly, Silent, Hostile. (Antonym) Cheerful.

Summit (noun) The highest point of a mountain.
▪ The climbers were happy when they finally reached the summit.
The highest level; meetings between leaders of two or more governments.
▪ Many heads of state attended the climate summit last year in New York City.
(Synonym) Peak, Conference, Meeting.

Sumptuous (adjective) Very expensive, rich, or impressive.
▪ The couple had a sumptuous reception at their wedding in Italy.
(Synonym) Luxurious, Lavish, Splendid.

Sunder (verb) To split apart, especially in a violent way; to become parted, disunited, or severed.
▪ Their marriage was sundered by an adulterous affair.
(Synonym) Separate, Divide, Split.

Superficial (adjective) Concerned only with what is obvious or apparent; without depth.
▪ The accident caused only superficial damage to the car's paint.
(Synonym) Shallow, Artificial, Unimportant. (Antonym) Sincere.

Superfluous (adjective) Beyond what is needed; exceeding what is sufficient; extra; not necessary.

▪ This information is superfluous.
(Synonym) Surplus, Redundant, Excessive. (Antonym) Basic.

Supplant (verb) To take the place of someone or something that is old or no longer used or accepted.
▪ Typewriters have been supplanted by personal computers.
(Synonym) Displace, Oust, Replace. (Antonym) Install.

Surly (adjective) Rude and unfriendly.
▪ She always has a surly remark for her rival.
(Synonym) Gruff, Brusque, Abrupt. (Antonym) Courteous.

Surmise (verb) To form an opinion about something without definitely knowing the truth; guess.
▪ When she saw the empty ice cream container, she surmised that her brother had eaten all of it.
(Synonym) Conclude, Assume, Infer.

Surrogate (noun) A person or thing that takes the place or performs the duties of someone or something else.
▪ The infertile couple used a surrogate mother in order to have children.
(Synonym) Substitute, Replacement, Proxy.

Susceptible (adjective) Easily affected, influenced, or harmed by something; open.
▪ Computers are very susceptible to viruses.
(Synonym) Vulnerable, Prone, Subject.

Sympathy (noun) The feeling that you care and are sorry about someone else's trouble, grief, misfortune.
▪ We sent the family a sympathy card after the death of their loved one.
(Synonym) Understanding, Compassion, Empathy. (Antonym) Incomprehension.

Synopsis (noun) A brief survey of something; a short description.
▪ The professor asked for a synopsis of the first chapter.
(Synonym) Outline, Summary, Abridgment.

Tacit (adjective) Without words or speech; implied by silence; not actually expressed.
▪ Emilie never asked to go to the party, but her parents gave her their tacit approval to do so.
(Synonym) Inferred, Understood, Implied. (Antonym) Explicit.

Taciturn (adjective) Tending to be quiet; not speaking frequently.
▪ Jill is a taciturn young woman who would rather read than converse.
(Synonym) Reserved, Silent, Aloof. (Antonym) Garrulous.

Taint (verb) To hurt or damage the good condition of something.
- After the scandal, the reputation of the university has been tainted.

To affect with putrefaction; spoil.
- The water had been tainted by pesticides.

(Synonym) Stain, Blemish, Infect. (Antonym) Enhance.

Talisman (noun) An object such as a ring or stone that is believed to have magic powers to avert evil and bring good fortune to the person who has it; something believed to bring good luck.
- I wore the sterling silver bracelet as a talisman of good health.

(Synonym) Jewel, Amulet, Charm.

Tangible (adjective) Easily seen or recognized; able to be touched or felt.
- I need tangible evidence to support the existence of aliens.

Capable of being appraised at an actual or approximate value.
- The corporation's tangible assets included a fleet of delivery trucks and numerous warehouses.

(Synonym) Palpable, Touchable, Perceptible.

Tardy (adjective) Delayed beyond the expected time.
- My teacher says that being tardy for class is never acceptable.

(Synonym) Slow, Late, Overdue. (Antonym) Punctual, Prompt.

Tarnish (verb) To become, or to cause metal to become, dull and not shiny.
- The silver ring is tarnished and needs cleaning.

To bring disgrace upon.
- The reputation of the university was tarnished by the scandal.

(Synonym) Damage, Stain, Taint. (Antonym) Clean.

Tattered (adjective) Old and torn; wearing ragged clothes.
- Three weeks after getting lost, she emerged from the rainforest wearing tattered clothes.

(Synonym) Dilapidated, Unkempt, Messy. (Antonym) Pristine.

Taunt (verb) To say insulting things to someone in order to make that person angry.
- The boys continually taunted the homeless man.

(Synonym) Provoke, Tease, Mock. (Antonym) Compliment.

Tawdry (adjective) Having a cheap, gaudy, and ugly appearance or quality; morally low or bad.
- The house is filled with tawdry decorations.

(Synonym) Tasteless, Garish, Crude. (Antonym) Tasteful.

Tedious (adjective) Tiresome because of length or dullness; boring and too slow.
- The lecturer gave a tedious speech.

(Synonym) Wearisome, Prolonged, Monotonous. (Antonym) Interesting.

Teem (verb) To be full of life and activity.
▪ The bay was teeming with fish, lobsters, and shrimp.
Sometimes used figuratively.
▪ His creative young mind is teeming with ideas.
(Synonym) Swarmed, Abounded, Poured. (Antonym) Dispersed.

Tell (verb) To communicate information, facts, or news to someone using speech or written words.
▪ She chose to tell the judge the facts of the case.
(Synonym) Express, Articulate, Divulge.

Temperate (adjective) Temperatures that are not too hot or too cold; marked by moderation; not extreme.
▪ They preferred the temperate climate of the mountains over the hot desert below.
Emotionally calm and controlled,
▪ He is temperate in his response to criticism.
(Synonym) Composed, Mild, Reasonable.

Tenacious (adjective) Not easily pulled apart; firm or strong; very determined to do something.
▪ Gilbert is courageous, tenacious, and passionate about helping people.
(Synonym) Stubborn, Obstinate, Unyielding. (Antonym) Irresolute.

Tentative (adjective) Not done with confidence; uncertain and hesitant; not definite; still able to be changed.
▪ The labor dispute was resolved in a tentative manner.
(Synonym) Uncertain, Cautious, Indefinite. (Antonym) Sure, Definite.

Tenuous (adjective) Not certain or definite; flimsy or weak.
▪ The defense's tenuous argument did not help them win the case.
(Synonym) Feeble, Fragile, Slender. (Antonym) Strong.

Terminate (verb) To end in a particular way; to take a job away from someone.
▪ The CEO terminated the employment of many employees in his company.
(Synonym) Fire, Lay off, Put an end to. (Antonym) Hire.

Terrain (noun) Land of a particular kind; a geographic area; a piece of land.
▪ The villagers had to cross over the rocky terrain to find water.
(Synonym) Landscape, Territory, Ground.

Terse (adjective) Brief and direct in a way that may seem rude or unfriendly; using few words.
▪ "Get out! I don't want to see you again!" Marie said tersely.
(Synonym) Concise, Succinct, Pointed. (Antonym) Rambling.

Therapeutic (adjective) Producing good effects on your body or mind.
▪ The therapeutic benefits of exercise have been demonstrated in many studies.

Of or relating to the treatment of disease or disorders by remedial agents or methods.
- Shopping can be a therapeutic activity for some.
(Synonym) Healing, Curative, Medicinal. (Antonym) Stressful.

Thesis (noun) A long piece of writing on a particular subject that is done to earn a degree at a university.
- Her thesis concerns capital punishment.
(Synonym) Theory, Argument, Belief.

Tic (noun) A small repeated movement of a muscle, especially in the face, that cannot be controlled.
- He was self-conscious about his facial tic.
A word or phrase that someone frequently says or an action that someone frequently does without intending to.
- He has had the tic in this foot his entire life.
(Synonym) Spasm, Twitch, Convulsion.

Timid (adjective) Feeling or showing a lack of courage or self-confidence; lacking in boldness or determination.
- Pierce is very timid and will not talk to strangers.
(Synonym) Nervous, Shy, Reticent. (Antonym) Bold.

Toil (noun) Work that is difficult and unpleasant and that lasts for a long time; long, hard labor.
- My grandmother spent days of toil and sweat in the cotton fields.
(Synonym) Work, Labor, Drudgery. (Antonym) Relaxation.

Token (noun) Something that is a symbol of a feeling or event.
- Please accept this gift as a token of my appreciation.
A round piece of metal or plastic that looks like a coin that is used instead of money in some machines.
- New York City did away with subway tokens several years ago in favor of Metro Cards.
(Synonym) Symbol, Coin, Mark.

Tolerance (noun) Sympathy or indulgence for feelings, habits, beliefs differing from or conflicting with one's own.
- The manager does not have tolerance for laziness and tardiness.
The ability to accept, experience, or survive something harmful or unpleasant.
- I do not have much tolerance for hot temperatures.
(Synonym) Lenience, Open-mindedness, Forbearance.

Toxic (adjective) Containing poisonous substances.
- The environmentalist warned that toxic chemicals from the proposed plant could contaminate air and water in the community.
(Synonym) Contaminated, Deadly, Lethal. (Antonym) Harmless.

Tracery (noun) Decorative patterns made in stone in some church windows.
- The church has a beautiful window decorated with Gothic tracery.
Lines that cross each other in a complicated and attractive pattern.
- The delicate silver tracery of the moonlight shone through the trees.
(Synonym) Pattern, Design, Ornamentation.

Tradition (noun) The stories or beliefs that have been part of the culture in a family or society for a long time.
- Though they are creative and celebrate originality, the students are sure to maintain the school traditions.
(Synonym) Custom, Ritual, Practice. (Antonym) Innovation.

Tragedy (noun) A very bad event that causes great sadness; a work of art that depicts tragic events.
- *Hamlet* is perhaps Shakespeare's best-known tragedy.
(Synonym) Disaster, Calamity, Misfortune. (Antonym) Joy.

Transcribe (verb) To make a written copy of something; to paraphrase or summarize in writing.
- He transcribed medical records for doctors.
To change something written into a different language.
- The company transcribes textbooks from English to French.
(Synonym) Record, Reproduce, Translate.

Transform (verb) A big change in form, appearance, or behavior.
- She transformed from a shy girl into a strong and respected young woman.
(Synonym) Renovate, Make over, Change.

Transgress (verb) To do something that is not allowed; to disobey a command or law. To go beyond a boundary or limit.
- She transgressed the school's rules by cheating.
(Synonym) Misbehave, Fall from grace, Violate.

Transmit (verb) To send information such as sound in the form of electrical signals to a radio, television, or computer; to cause or allow to spread; to send out a signal either by radio waves or over a wire.
- Today, new technology allows us to transmit messages faster.
(Synonym) Convey, Communicate, Broadcast.

Travail (noun) A difficult experience or situation; painful or difficult work or effort.
- My grandmother spent days of travail in the cotton fields.
(Synonym) Drudgery, Toil, Labor.

Travesty (noun) Something that is shocking, upsetting, or ridiculous because it is not what it is supposed to be.
- It is a travesty of justice that the judge let the killer go free.

(Synonym) Charade, Mockery, Farce.

Tread (verb) To step or walk on or over.
- The children are treading on the grass instead of using the walkway.
(Synonym) Footstep, Tramp, Plod.

Tremendous (adjective) Very large or great; very good or excellent; wonderful.
- It was with tremendous joy that I received my increase in salary.
(Synonym) Marvelous, Enormous, Huge. (Antonym) Tiny.

Trepidation (noun) A feeling of fear that causes you to hesitate because you think something unpleasant is going to happen.
- Jonas felt nervous trepidation the night before the final history exam.
(Synonym) Apprehension, Anxiety, Concern. (Antonym) Equanimity.

Triathlon (noun) A long-distance race that has three parts such as swimming, bicycling, and running.
- She won the bronze medal In the Olympic triathlon despite having crashed her bicycle.

Tribute (noun) A gift or service showing respect, gratitude, or affection for someone.
- The concert was to pay tribute to the veterans.
A payment by one ruler or nation to another in acknowledgment of submission or as the price of protection.
- The country was forced to pay tribute to its militaristic neighbor.
(Synonym) Compliment, Honor, Praise.

Trite (adjective) Not interesting or effective because of being used too often; not fresh or original.
- The story may sound trite and hackneyed, but it is true.
(Synonym) Common, Corny, Banal. (Antonym) Original.

Trivial (adjective) Not important; of little worth or importance.
- The gang members are fighting over trivial issues.
(Synonym) Small, Insignificant, Petty. (Antonym) Crucial.

Truce (noun) An agreement between enemies to stop fighting for a certain period of time.
- The two countries broke the truce.
(Synonym) Treaty, Pause Respite.

Truncate (verb) To make something shorter.
- The teacher advised me to truncate my essay by at least two paragraphs.
(Synonym) Shorten, Abbreviate, Cut. (Antonym) Lengthen.

Trying (adjective) Difficult to deal with, annoying.
▪ My little sister can be very trying at times; she does everything I tell her not to.
(Synonym) Demanding, Irritating, Strenuous.

Tumult (noun) A loud, confusing noise.
▪ The tumult in the street made people lock their doors and pull down their curtains.
(Synonym) Mayhem, Commotion, Disorder.

Turbulent (adjective) Causing unrest, violence, or disturbance.
▪ He is an unruly child with turbulent moods.
Characterized by agitation or tumult; not stable or steady.
▪ The sixties were a turbulent period in US history.
(Synonym) Stormy, Tempestuous, Unstable. (Antonym) Settled.

QUIZ 11.- MATCH EACH WORD IN THE FIRST COLUMN WITH ITS SYNONYM IN THE SECOND COLUMN. CHECK YOUR ANSWERS IN THE BACK OF THE BOOK.

1. satiate	a. land
2. scarce	b. concise
3. skeptic	c. silent
4. sluggish	d. touchable
5. spectrum	e. labor
6. succinct	f. curative
7. summit	g. violent
8. synopsis	h. of little importance
9. taciturn	i. satisfy
10. tangible	j. rare
11. terrain	k. summary
12. therapeutic	l. conference
13. travail	m. range
14. trivial	n. doubter
15. turbulent	o. slow

Turmoil (noun) A state or condition of extreme confusion, agitation, disorder, or commotion.
▪ The school cafeteria was engulfed in turmoil when the seniors started a food fight.
(Synonym) Chaos, Mayhem, Uproar.

Tycoon (noun) A businessperson of exceptional wealth and power; a top leader as in politics.
▪ The Greek tycoon owned shipping companies, television and radio stations, and a distillery.
(Synonym) Magnate, Mogul, Industrialist.

Typical (adjective) Normal for a person, thing, or group; happening in the usual way.
▪ We had a typical New England winter: cold and snowy.
(Synonym) Characteristic, Distinctive, Representative. (Antonym) Unusual.

Ulcer (noun) A painful sore area inside or outside the body.
▪ She suffers from a stomach ulcer and must take a medication daily.
(Synonym) Boil, Abscess, Pustule.

Ultimate (adjective) Happening or coming at the end of a process or series of events; greatest or most extreme.
▪ Annabeth's ultimate goal is to open a preparatory school.
(Synonym) Final, Decisive, Vital.

Ultimatum (noun) A final threat; a promise that punishment will be used if someone does not do what is wanted.
▪ His father gave him an ultimatum: "Go to college or leave the house."
(Synonym) Last word, Proposition, Challenge.

Unblushing (adjective) Not blushing; shameless.
▪ Even though Anna fell down the stairs in front of her peers, she unblushingly continued on her way as though nothing had happened.

Unflinching (adjective) Not showing fear in the face of danger or difficulty.
▪ Soldiers are trained to be unflinching when faced with difficult situations.
(Synonym) Uncompromising, Dogged, Determined.

Unfurl (verb) To cause something that is folded or rolled up to open.
▪ It is difficult to unfurl a sail in strong winds.
(Synonym) Expand, Open up, Spread out.

Uniform (noun) A special kind of clothing that is worn by all the members of a group; staying the same at all time.
▪ The school uniforms were dark green and with yellow accents.
(Synonym) Sameness, Evenness, Monotony.

Unkempt (adjective) Not neat or orderly; messy or untidy.
▪ Stacy's poorly washed and unkempt hair made her unappealing to the boys in her class.
(Synonym) Slovenly, Raggedy, Disorganized. (Antonym) Neat.

Unlettered (adjective) Unable to read or write.
▪ Sarah's unlettered maid found it difficult to use a cookbook unless it was copiously illustrated.
(Synonym) Uneducated, Illiterate, Unschooled.

Unnumbered (adjective) Not marked or assigned a number.

▪ We need to mark the unnumbered boxes before shipping them off.
(Synonym) Unidentified, Numberless, Countless.

Unscrupulous (adjective) Not honest or fair; doing things that are wrong, dishonest, or illegal.
▪ The unscrupulous student steals other students' lunch money.
(Synonym) Corrupt, Unprincipled, Immoral. (Antonym) Honest.

Untimely (adjective) Happening or done sooner than you expect; occurring before the proper or right time.
▪ I am saddened by the news of my friend's untimely death.
(Synonym) Premature, Early, Inappropriate. (Antonym) Late.

Unusual (adjective) Not normal or usual; not commonly seen or heard.
▪ The color of his hair was an unusual shade of red and blue.
(Synonym) Rare, Unfamiliar, Peculiar.

Utility (noun) The quality or state of being useful.
▪ I question the utility of a winter coat if you are moving to Florida.
A service such as electricity, water, and natural gas that is provided to the public.
▪ The bills for utilities are too high this month; we need to conserve energy.
(Synonym) Practicality, Usefulness, Value. (Antonym) Worthlessness.

Utilize (verb) To use something for a particular purpose.
▪ The students need to utilize the resources in the school's library.
(Synonym) Exploit, Employ, Make use of. (Antonym) Forgo.

Vacant (adjective) Not occupied by an incumbent; not filled, used, or lived in.
▪ There were no vacant apartments in the building.
(Synonym) Empty, Available, Stark. (Antonym) Occupied.

Vague (adjective) Not clearly expressed; not clear in meaning; not specific.
▪ She has been vague about her plans for college.
(Synonym) Imprecise, Ambiguous, Nebulous. (Antonym) Clear.

Vain (adjective) Without success; without producing a good or desired result; marked by futility.
▪ We searched in vain for the missing earring.
To use a name, especially the name of God, in a way that does not show proper respect.
▪ Some religions consider it sinful to take God's name in vain.
(Synonym) Otiose, Ineffective, Conceited. (Antonym) Successful.

Valet (noun) A man's servant who performs personal services; a person who parks cars for guests at a hotel or restaurant; standing rack for holding clothing.
▪ A valet parked my car while I entered the restaurant.
(Synonym) Butler, Retainer, Footman.

Valor (noun) Strength of mind that enables a person to encounter danger with firmness; courage or personal bravery.
- The president presented the soldier with the nation's highest award for valor, the Medal of Honor.
(Synonym) Gallantry, Heroism, Boldness. (Antonym) Cowardice.

Vault (verb) Spring over, jump.

Vault (noun) An arched structure that forms a ceiling or roof.
- The tourists gazed up at the vault of the cathedral and took pictures.
A locked room where money or valuable things are kept.
- The thieves were thwarted by the bank vault's construction.
(Synonym) Dome, Treasury, Leap.

Venerable (adjective) Valued and respected because of old age or long use.
- He's the community's venerable bishop.
(Synonym) Honored, Revered, Admired. (Antonym) Disreputable.

Veracious (adjective) Truthful; speaking the truth as a matter of course.
- The defense was thrilled to find a veracious witness.
(Synonym) Honest, Reliable, Genuine. (Antonym) Dishonest.

Verbose (adjective) Using more words than are needed.
- Students need to be concise in their writing; they should take care that their writing style is not verbose.
(Synonym) Talkative, Wordy, Loquacious. (Antonym) Taciturn.

Verdict (noun) The decision made by a jury in a trial.
- The jury could not reach a verdict after days of deliberation, so the judge declared a mistrial.
(Synonym) Judgment, Result, Outcome.

Verify (verb) Make sure or demonstrate that something is true or correct.
- Her job was to verify that the toys were properly labeled.
(Synonym) Confirm, Prove, Validate.

Versatile (adjective) Able to do many different things; having many different uses.
- She is a versatile musician who plays several string and wind instruments.
(Synonym) Adaptable, Flexible, Multitalented. (Antonym) Limited.

Vessel (noun) A container like a bowl or cask, especially used to hold liquid.
- Each vessel holds a different type of tea.
(Synonym) Bowl, Pitcher, Container.

Vestige (noun) The last small part that remains of something that existed before.
- The earthquake left only vestiges of the ancient cathedral.
(Synonym) Remnant, Trace, Evidence.

Veto (noun) A decision by a person in authority to not allow or approve something such as a new law.
- A presidential veto can be used to block the enactment of legislation.
(Synonym) Refusal, Censure, Rejection. (Antonym) Approval, Release.

Vex (verb) To annoy or worry.
- I vexed my friend until she gave me the answers to the questions.
(Synonym) Irritate, Aggravate, Upset.

Vie (verb) To compete with others in an attempt to get or win something.
- She placed second in the competition, but she was vying for the blue ribbon.
(Synonym) Compete, Contend, Oppose. (Antonym) Collaborate.

Vigilant (adjective) Carefully noticing problems or signs of danger.
- When taking the subway, we should be vigilant and remain aware of our surroundings.
(Synonym) Watchful, Alert, Observant. (Antonym) Oblivious, Slack.

Vigorous (adjective) Healthy and strong; done with great force and energy.
- My grandmother remained vigorous and active into her late nineties.
(Synonym) Dynamic, Vital, Robust. (Antonym) Sluggish, Lethargic.

Vintage (adjective) Wine usually of high quality that was produced in a particular year, which is identified on the bottle.
- The restaurant served only vintage wines at my sister's wedding.
Used to describe something that is not new but that is valued because of its good condition, attractive design, etc.
- I bought a vintage bag at the thrift store.
(Synonym) Out of date, Antique, Traditional. (Antonym) New.

Visage (noun) A person's face; appearance of a person.
- She has a smiling visage.
(Synonym) Look, Appearance, Face.

Vivacious (adjective) Happy and lively in a way that is attractive—used especially of a woman.
- Elizabeth has a warm and vivacious personality.
(Synonym) Vibrant, Effervescent, Animated. (Antonym) Languid.

Volition (noun) The power to make your own choices or decisions.
- He broke the law of his own volition; no one forced him to drive without a license.
(Synonym) Will, Desire, Option. (Antonym) Coercion.

Voluble (adjective) Talking a lot in an energetic and rapid way; characterized by ready or rapid speech.
- Gilbert is a voluble speaker; sometimes it is hard to get him to shut up.

(Synonym) Articulate, Talkative, Garrulous. (Antonym) Taciturn.

Voracious (adjective) Having a very eager approach to an activity; wanting great quantities of food; excessively eager.
- My professor described me as a voracious reader; I read everything I can get my hands on.
(Synonym) Avid, Hungry, Gluttonous.

Vouch (verb) To say that someone is honest, true, or good; to summon into court; to warrant or defend a title.
- I can vouch for her good character; she is always kind and reliable.
(Synonym) Guarantee, Swear, Assure.

Vow (noun) Serious promise to do something or to behave in a certain way.
- The bride and groom exchanged vows to care for each other "till death do us part."
(Synonym) Oath, Pledge, Declaration.

Vulgar (adjective) Lacking in cultivation, perception, or good taste; relating to the speech of common people.
- The school punished my friends for using crude and vulgar language.
(Synonym) Rude, Crude, Ill-mannered.

Vulnerable (adjective) Capable of being physically or emotionally wounded; open to attack, harm, or damage.
- Computers are vulnerable to viruses.
(Synonym) Susceptible, Weak, Defenseless. (Antonym) Invincible.

Vulture (noun) Any one of several large birds that eat dead animals and have a small and featherless head; a rapacious or predatory person who tries to take advantage of someone who is in a very bad situation.
- As soon as they learned of the princess's death, the media vultures started circling.
(Synonym) Predator, Scavenger, Shark.

Waft (verb) To move or go lightly through the air or by the impulse of wind or waves.
- A breeze wafted the scent of lavender up to my bedroom window.
(Synonym) Blow, Float, Drift.

Waive (verb) To officially say that you will not use something that you are allowed to have or that is usually required.
- The independent school waives the application fee for low-income students.
(Synonym) Relinquish, Give up, Renounce.

Wan (adjective) Looking sick or pale; having a weak quality.
- Lucy looks tired and wan; she has been overworking herself lately.
(Synonym) Ashen, Listless, Feeble. (Antonym) Strong.

Wanton (adjective) Showing no thought or care for the rights, feelings, or safety of others.
- The company showed a wanton disregard for its employees' well-being.
Having no real provocation or justification; malicious.
- Wanton attack.
Causing sexual excitement; lustful, sensual.
(Synonym) Cruel, Immoral, Malevolent.

Wariness (noun) Not having complete trust in someone who could be dangerous or cause trouble.
- The security guard expressed wariness about the suspicious customer who entered the store.
(Synonym) Suspicion, Circumspection, Caution.

Weird (adjective) Unusual; of strange or extraordinary character; odd; fantastic.
- The jazz band made weird sounds at the concert.
(Synonym) Eerie, Bizarre, Peculiar. (Antonym) Normal.

Wharf (noun) A flat structure that is built along the shore of a river, ocean, so that ships can load and unload.
- Arnold worked on the canal wharf for most of his life.
(Synonym) Quay, Pier, Dock, Waterfront.

Wheedle (verb) To persuade by flattery or cajolery; to influence or entice by soft words.
- She tried in vain to wheedle the teacher into giving her a better grade for the test.
(Synonym) Coax, Persuade, Obtain. (Antonym) Bully.

Whim (noun) A sudden wish, desire, decision.
- My sister is capricious; she wants us to satisfy her every whim.
(Synonym) Impulse, Urge, Caprice.

Whimsical (adjective) Unusual in a playful or amusing way; not serious.
- She displays whimsical behavior.
(Synonym) Creative, Quirky, Impulsive. (Antonym) Practical, Serious.

Wily (adjective) Full of clever tricks; very clever.
- Adam's wily opponents were able to win the negotiation.
(Synonym) Cunning, Astute, Lumpy. (Antonym) Ingenuous, Open.

Winsome (adjective) Cheerful, pleasant, and appealing often because of a childlike charm and innocence.
- My son has a winning, winsome manner; his charm never fails to endear him to his peers.
(Synonym) Charming, Attractive, Engaging. (Antonym) Repellent.

Wither (verb) To become dry and shriveled; lose vigor, vitality, freshness or importance.
- When I came back from vacation, I discovered that the plants in my kitchen had withered and died.
(Synonym) Decline, Fade, Wilt. (Antonym) Strengthen, Bloom.

QUIZ 12.- MATCH EACH WORD IN THE FIRST COLUMN WITH ITS SYNONYM IN THE SECOND COLUMN. CHECK YOUR ANSWERS IN THE BACK OF THE BOOK.

1. unkempt		a. face
2. unusual		b. charming
3. utilize		c. peak
4. vacant		d. wordy
5. valor		e. adaptable
6. venerable		f. prove
7. veracious		g. trace
8. verbose		h. give up
9. verify		i. messy
10. versatile		j. courage
11. vestige		k. make use of
12. visage		l. peculiar
13. waive		m. stark
14. winsome		n. true
15. zenith		o. respected

Woeful (adjective) Full of woe; very sad; lamentably bad or serious; deplorable.
▪ The students looked woeful as they read the syllabus with the list of assignments due next month.
(Synonym) Unhappy, Wretched, Pathetic. (Antonym) Cheerful.

Wreak (verb) To express vengeance or punishment; to cause harm and damage.
▪ Recently, gangs have been wreaking havoc on the south side of Chicago.
(Synonym) Inflict, Carry out, Unleash.

Writ (noun) An order or mandatory process in the legal system; a piece of writing issued in the name of the sovereign or of a court or judicial officer commanding the person to whom it is directed to perform or refrain from performing an act specified therein.
(Synonym) Summons, Injunction, Court order.

Writhe (verb) To twist one's body from side to side; to twist so as to distort.
▪ Michael laid on the athletic field writhing in pain.
(Synonym) Squirm, Wriggle, Struggle.

Yearn (verb) To feel a strong desire or wish for something; to long for persistently, wistfully, or sadly.
▪ People are yearning for freedom.
(Synonym) Desire, Crave, Thirst.

Zeal (noun) A strong feeling of interest and enthusiasm.
▪ She attacked her homework with renewed zeal after getting her first A.
(Synonym) Enthusiasm, Passion, Fervor. (Antonym) Apathy.

Zenith (noun) The strongest or most successful period of time; the highest point.
▪ At its zenith, the band played more than thirty concerts in a month.
(Synonym) Peak, Summit, Apogee. (Antonym) Nadir.

Zephyr (noun) A very slight or gentle wind; a breeze from the west; lightweight fabrics.
▪ A gentle zephyr rustled the curtains.
(Synonym) Gentle wind, Light wind, Puff of air.

Zest (noun) A lively quality that increases enjoyment, enthusiasm, excitement, and energy.
▪ She works with zest and is a positive example to her coworkers.
A piece of the peel of a citrus fruit as an orange or lemon used to flavor food.
▪ I cooked my oatmeal with a tablespoon of lemon zest.
(Synonym) Passion, Relish, Taste. (Antonym) Apathy.

The answers

QUIZ #1	QUIZ #2	QUIZ #3	QUIZ #4
1. e	1. c	1. f	1. e
2. k	2. k	2. l	2. c
3. h	3. h	3. e	3. i
4. f	4. m	4. m	4. o
5. i	5. n	5. b	5. b
6. n	6. o	6. g	6. h
7. o	7. d	7. c	7. n
8. a	8. j	8. n	8. j
9. m	9. b	9. j	9. f
10. g	10. l	10. h	10. k
11. l	11. g	11. o	11. a
12. c	12. f	12. i	12. m
13. j	13. a	13. k	13. g
14. b	14. i	14. a	14. l
15. d	15. e	15. d	15. d

The Answers

QUIZ # 5	QUIZ # 6	QUIZ # 7	QUIZ 8
1. c	1. e	1. c	1. c
2. k	2. f	2. j	2. d
3. f	3. j	3. a	3. g
4. m	4. k	4. k	4. i
5. b	5. l	5. h	5. m
6. o	6. h	6. m	6. h
7. l	7. b	7. i	7. k
8. e	8. m	8. n	8. a
9. n	9. c	9. o	9. o
10. h	10. o	10. d	10. f
11. a	11. d	11. e	11. j
12. j	12. n	12. g	12. b
13. d	13. g	13. f	13. n
14. i	14. a	14. l	14. e
15. g	15. i	15. b	15. l

QUIZ #9	QUIZ #10	QUIZ #11	QUIZ #12
1. g	1. f	1. i	1. i
2. k	2. d	2. j	2. l
3. n	3. j	3. n	3. k
4. h	4. h	4. o	4. m
5. i	5. m	5. m	5. j
6. j	6. n	6. b	6. o
7. o	7. c	7. l	7. n
8. e	8. l	8. k	8. d
9. b	9. k	9. c	9. f
10. a	10. a	10. d	10. e
11. l	11. o	11. a	11. g
12. m	12. i	12. f	12. a
13. f	13. b	13. e	13. h
14. d	14. g	14. h	14. b
15. c	15. e	15. g	15. c

Bibliography

Merriam-Webster, Incorporated. *Learners Dictionary*. Online Dictionary. "http://www.learnersdictionary.com".

Jewell, Elizabeth J. *Pocket Oxford Dictionary & Thesaurus: Second American Edition.* Oxford University Press, 2002

Made in the USA
Middletown, DE
14 April 2017